"This compelling dialogue between two Catholic priest-theologians, Thomas Berry and Thomas Clarke, progresses in a profound sense of the radical breakdown of the cultural and socio-economic systems that have dominated the West for several millennia. The proliferation of human population on the globe literally threatens planetary life itself. Berry and Clarke reflect on the terror we must learn to experience as the magnitude of this disaster becomes clear, but also on the way forward to a new life-sustaining community. Most of all, they ask what is salvageable and what must be discarded in Christianity in order to guide us through this transition. Berry and Clarke give voice to the issues that all humans on earth must begin to discuss in the last decade of the twentieth century."

Rosemary Radford Ruether
Garrett-Evangelical Theological Seminary

"*Befriending the Earth* is an exceptionally helpful introduction to the thought of 'geologian' Thomas Berry, certainly one of this century's most significant thinkers. This book (and the accompanying videotape series) is a goldmine of prophetic insight and inspiration. For those concerned or curious about the direction of Christianity in the third millennium, this book is a must!"

Michael Dowd, Author
Earthspirit: A Handbook for Nurturing an Ecological Christianity

"I have enjoyed *Befriending the Earth* thoroughly. The dialogue between Thomas Berry and Thomas Clarke offers a paradigm of the way theological discussion should be done. It is obvious that their dialogue is rooted in profound respect, and although two some what different worlds are meeting, the resul ters of both theology and science are enriched

"It is no accident that the word 'revelatory frequently recurring words. There is much here: of new insights into old traditions and that shed new light on old unfinished dialogue

Mary T. Malone
University of St. Jerome's College
Waterloo, Ontario

"Few authors have the depth of wisdom, intuitive vision, and intellectual radiance of Thomas Berry and Thomas Clarke. In *Befriending the Earth,* Thomas Berry, a major contributor to the growing link between healthy spirituality and ecology, clarifies his thoughts in this profoundly simple yet brilliant book.

"In dialogue with Thomas Clarke, Berry presents his thoughts in what I can only describe as a universal catechism that takes seriously the fact that the universe itself is a sacred community, made of the very stuff of God. Tom Berry points the way for all religious travelers, Christian, Buddhist, Hindu, etc., who hope to have the earth under their feet in the future.

"*Befriending the Earth* has left me stunned with terror at the ravages we have inflicted on the earth and her biosystems, ashamed at the ignorance of the Christian tradition that has actually fostered such blasphemy, yet healthier with the knowledge that the human community may have the courage—if not the time—to dramatically change the way we live on planet earth."

John Powers, C.P.
Author, *Holy Human: Mystics for Our Time*

"This edition of the proceedings of the Port Burwell conference is magnificent. The dialogue between Berry and Clarke has a depth and range unequaled. Berry's work constitutes one of the most far-reaching analysis of our times. Father Clarke's reflections on Berry's work and their interchange are profound, indeed. Their reflections in *Befriending the Earth* represent a distillation of all of the major issues that face us today in our civilizational crisis. Their reflections have a depth and range that is not likely to be surpassed."

Dr. Edmund Sullivan
The Ontario Institute for Studies in Education

"*Befriending the Earth* represents one of the most important contributions in the newly emerging field of religion and ecology. It can be used with profit by those seeking to engender a renewed sense of reverence for all forms of life. The dialogue between Berry and Clarke highlights the distinctive contribution of Berry's new cosmology and points to new directions for future theology."

Mary Evelyn Tucker,
Bucknell University, Lewisburg, Pennsylvania

Befriending the Earth

A Theology of Reconciliation
Between Humans and the Earth

Thomas Berry, C.P.
in dialogue with
Thomas Clarke, S.J.

Stephen Dunn, C.P. and Anne Lonergan
Editors

TWENTY-THIRD PUBLICATIONS
Mystic, Connecticut

Twenty-Third Publications
185 Willow Street
P.O. Box 180
Mystic, CT 06355
(203) 536-2611

ISBN 0-89622-471-6
Library of Congress Catalog Card No. 90-71817

Acknowledgments

This book is, more than most, the work of a community, beginning with Thomas Berry and the Passionists of Canada, who have collaborated at Holy Cross Centre in Port Burwell, Ontario, for twelve years, shaping an institution for spirituality and ecology. The staff, Paul Cusack, Mary Margaret Howard, Stephen Paul Kenny, Lynda Nevins, Frank Casey, Brian Hamilton, as well as associates and friends, the Vella-Zarbs, Palmira Murphy, Jane Blewett, Lou Niznik, Lea Grevstad, Ted Landry, Maureen Landry-Barber, and Margot King, all contributed to this volume and the televised colloquium from which it emerged.

When Dawn MacDonald entered the life of the Centre in 1989, little did we know that whirlwind warnings were in effect on the shores of Lake Erie. As editor of the *Catholic Church Extension* magazine, she immediately commissioned an article on the Centre written by Gail Burns; she made invaluable links for us with other organizations, and finally organized and co-produced for Canada's VISION TV the thirteen-part series of the 1990 Centre Colloquium with Thomas Berry and Thomas Clarke. The television production itself was made possible by the generosity of the Vision network itself, and by the filming crew, headed by Jim Hanley and Jackie Barley. They were extremely adaptable and sensitive to the audience gathered for the event. In addition, their enthusiasm for the whole project, and their swift and successful video editing, was both inspiring and encouraging.

We are pleased that Twenty-Third Publications has continued its interest in Thomas Berry's work and in our Centre. Through the years, Neil and Pat Kluepfel have become dear friends and unwavering promoters for Thomas Berry's ideas. We also especially thank Stephen Scharper for his patience as we struggled to change our status as techno-peasants to that of semi-literate computer users.

Finally, we wish to thank our dialogue partners. We had read a thoughtful review of creation theology by Thomas Clarke, published in the December 1988 issue of *The Way*. Father Clarke's close friend, Jane Blewett, had encouraged him to consider the need for more extensive dialogue between Thomas Berry and mainstream theology. We approached him, and although we knew some of his work, we had no idea of the breadth, openness, frankness, and graciousness of Thomas Clarke in person. At a time when many have difficulty with church institutions, to witness two Roman Catholic priests, one Passionist, one Jesuit, bring their maturity, breadth of scholarship and vision together was an experience that left all of us in the audience both humbled and challenged.

Anne Lonergan and Stephen Dunn

DEDICATION

To St. Gerard Grace Dunn
and Alma Gaudet Lonergan
who first taught us what it means
to love the earth.

Contents

Introduction

Love all of God's creation, the whole and every grain of sand in it. Love every leaf, every ray of God's light. Love the animals, love the plants, love everything. If you love everything, you will perceive the divine mystery in things. (Fyodor Dostoyevsky, *The Brothers Karamazov*)

Ideas remain impractical when we have not grasped or been grasped by them. When we do not get an idea, we ask "how" to put it into practice, thereby trying to turn the insights of the soul into actions of the ego. But when an insight or idea has sunk in, practice invisibly changes. The idea has opened the eye of the soul. By seeing differently, we do differently....The only legitimate How? in regard to these psychological insights is: "How can I grasp an idea?" (James Hillman, *Re-Visioning Psychology*)

Thomas Berry, a cultural historian, has for many years explored the religious traditions of the world and the scientific tradition of the past few centuries. He is himself influenced by the work of Pierre Teilhard de Chardin (1881-1955) and, like him, concerned to heal the divorce between science and religion through an understanding of the cosmos as the primary, revelatory reality through space and time. He has been a "prophet in the wilderness" for many years, signaling the deep ecological crisis created, not only by our economic systems, but by our worldviews which have fostered an understanding of ourselves as the supreme reality and value of the earth, and all other species as having value only in their utility to ourselves.

1

Thomas Clarke has taught extensively in the area of spiritual theology and, like Berry, has a profound interest in culture. He has been involved in social justice efforts and liberation theology and makes links throughout the book between these issues and ecology.

The topics of this book are among the traditional topics of Roman Catholic theology: God, Trinity, creation, redemption, evil, grace, christology, sacrifice, sacraments, the role of the human, ritual, and spiritual discipline, to name a few salient themes. Berry, who calls himself a "conservative Christian," is renamed by Clarke a "radical conservative." We quote from Clarke: "After spending some time going through some of Tom Berry's works, it occurs to me, as an 'orthodox' theologian. . .that Tom has given us a system that is not only brilliant, which is obvious, but which at least from my limited perspective is quite congruous with the Judaeo-Christian heritage, which is part of Tom Berry's own background."

We present the topics in sections. An introduction, written by Anne Lonergan, with the assistance of Dawn McDonald's notes from the video series, is included in each chapter, as are discussion questions, which arose in part as Fathers Berry and Clarke shared their faith, hope, charity, and vision.

These reflections grew out of a conversation, rather than a formal theological dialogue. As a result, they in no way represent a definitive statement on the highly complex question of the relationship between Christian theology and ecology. They are, rather, preliminary thoughts on what the contours of a theology of reconciliation between humans and the earth might look like. We hope the conversation continues through this publication and the thirteen-part *Befriending the Earth* video series, also available from Twenty-Third Publications.

CHAPTER ONE

The Divine and Our Present Revelatory Moment

IN THIS CHAPTER, Berry claims that we are at the end of one biological age, the Cenozoic, and are moving into another, which he terms the "Ecozoic" period. This momentous change in our relationship with the planet requires that all human institutions be re-thought. Twentieth-century science has brought us to a sense of a time-developmental universe, in which we are seen to be descendants of and cousins to everything else in the universe. In addition, our patterns of relating to the rest of the universe as objects, rather than subjects, are criticized in light of our enormous ecological crisis.

Berry views the sense of God as separate from creation, or transcendent, as one of the chief difficulties of the Christian tradition. Earlier peoples of earth believed that the divine was pervasive, revealed in all of the natural world. Gradually, however, the idea of immanence was joined by the idea of transcendence. In the biblical world, first the Hebrews, then the Christians, began to see God as singular, male, and separate from nature, somewhere above and beyond the earth. Berry has written that an emphasis on transcendence weakened our sense of the sacred in the natural world and has become the context for our use and abuse of the planet. In academic Christian theology, the idea of immanence continues.

The re-thinking of theology begins with ideas of God and creation. Previous generations knew creation in a spatial universe, which was always renewing itself but not developing. Instead of a *cosmos*, we now have *cosmogenesis;* our universe has moved from *being* to *becoming*. Berry considers this a new revelatory moment, qualitatively different from biblical revelation, but certainly revelatory of how the divine operates in the universe. From his understanding of the process of cosmogenesis, Berry proposes a new model of the Trinity.

Thomas Clarke responds appreciatively to Berry's "synthetic" theological approach, and notes that Berry's reluctance to use the word "God" is in keeping with the best of the Christian tradition. Clarke explores the traditional meaning of God and creation, noting that, properly understood, transcendence might still be a useful term in the context of cosmogenesis. Both theologians view "Christian animism" as an important new concept for theology to engage, and they appreciate the contribution of the First Peoples, or native peoples, to an understanding of a deeper, more reverent sense of the divine as it is revealed in the natural world.

THOMAS BERRY

The Context

The Order of Magnitude of Our Situation

First we should discuss the order of magnitude of the events taking place in our times. What is happening in our times is not just another historical transition or simply another cultural change. The devastation of the planet that we are bringing about is negating some hundreds of millions, even billions, of years of past development on the earth. This is a most momentous period of change, a change unparalleled in the four and a half billion years of earth history.

Even as we reflect on what is happening, we need to reflect also on who we are and why we are faced with such a momentous issue. All indications suggest that we are, in a sense, a chosen group, a chosen generation, or a chosen human community. We did not ask to be here at this time. We were destined to be here at this time in the sense that the time of our lives is determined for us. Some of the prophets, when asked to undertake certain missions, said, "Don't choose me; that's too much for me." God says, "You are going anyway." We are not asked whether we wish to live at this particular time. We are here. The inescapable is before us.

My generation has lived through a large part of this momentous period of change. Public radio did not exist when I was born. To have gone through all the discoveries of science, to have seen the planet change as much as it has been changed, is stupendous. But we have changed not simply the human, not simply Western civilization, not simply the North American world, we have changed the very structure of the planet. We have changed the chemistry of the planet, the biosystems of the planet, even the geology of the planet. Now we are changing the ozone layer, and bringing about what is called the greenhouse effect.

Events in this modality and at this order of magnitude have never taken place in the total course of human history, possibly in the course of earth history. There have been significant moments of extinction at the end of the Paleozoic, some 220 million years ago, and also 65 million years ago at the end of the Mesozoic. But now we are in the terminal phase of the Cenozoic, a period when many of the developments of the past 65 million years are being extinguished. We are not capable of extinguishing everything, but we are wreaking severe damage on the earth process. We have even set in motion forces that are extinguishing many of the major life systems that have come into being during the Cenozoic period.

We could call this Cenozoic period, the last 65 million years, the "lyric" period of earth history. During this period, we have the full development of the flowers; we have the wondrous development of the birds and the insects. Many of these living forms

5

existed before the beginning of the Cenozoic but they had their full flowering only in the past 65 million years. Then we humans came into being. What we are doing is setting a reversed sequence of forces into operation. The whole Cenozoic process is to some extent being negated. What is happening is on *this* order of magnitude. What is happening is not simply something that is happening to the Western world, nor is it happening simply to the human. It is happening on a planetary scale.

All the human modalities of being that have existed in the past are being profoundly altered. We ourselves are being changed. Christianity, which came into being some 2000 years ago, and our biblical revelation, which began some 3500 years ago, must now function within this context at this order of magnitude. Unfortunately, there is no indication so far that Christians are beginning to think of this scale of change. Just as the planet is changing more than it has changed in such a long period of time, so the human order that brought about this change is being called to alter itself in an equally profound way. That is why I suggest that what is happening now to Christian theology, or any theology or any religious life or any moral code, is the most profound change that has taken place during the past 5000 years. All human affairs are forced to change more than they have changed, certainly since the larger civilizations came into being.

We can even say that all the civilizations and religious traditions which began generally 5000 years ago have accomplished a major part of their historical mission. This includes Christian civilization. It includes the total religious experience of the human. It includes all experience of the human. We can never do without these accomplishments. They will have a major role in shaping the future. But they have to change on an order in which they have never changed before. Teilhard de Chardin (1881-1955) gave expression to the greatest transformation in Christian thought since the time of St. Paul.

Sometimes I say it this way: The traditional religions in themselves and out of their existing resources cannot deal with the problems that we have to deal with, but we cannot deal with these problems without the traditions. They cannot do it within their own resources as they exist at the present time, but it cannot be done without them. Something new has been added, a new experience, a new context, and we must now function out of this new context. We cannot deductively get our guidance from the past. There is, in a sense, a new revelatory experience that has given us a new sense of the universe, a new sense of the planet earth, a new sense of life, of the human, even a new sense of being Christian. We have, in a sense, a new revelatory experience of the divine through our present understanding of the time-developmental universe.

The universe story is the quintessence of reality. We perceive the story. We put it in our language, the birds put it in theirs, and the trees put it in theirs. We can read the story of the universe in the trees. Everything tells the story of the universe. The winds tell the story, literally, not just imaginatively. The story has its imprint everywhere, and that is why it is so important to know the story. If you do not know the story, in a certain sense you do not know yourself; you do not know anything.

Our Time-Developmental Universe as Revelatory

Revelation is the awakening in the depth of human psychic awareness of a sense of ultimate mystery and how ultimate mystery communicates itself. Take the prophets. When they talked about revelation, they used the term "God sayeth," but did they hear or see something? God? Surely no one can see or hear God. In reality, they did not hear anything audible or see anything visible, but they did become aware in the depths of their being of a special type of divine communication. This came from a depth beyond anything that they could envisage as coming from a created origin. And so, "God sayeth" is a special interior depth of awareness. The same is true with our situation. When I call our new knowledge of the universe a new revelatory experience, it is qualitatively different, just as all revelatory experiences are qualitatively different.

We cannot say, for example, that the Hindu world did not experience revelation. They themselves were very conscious of receiving a revelation. Faith is a primary word in all the traditions.

Even among scientists, there is a growing awareness of the trans-scientific implications of science. There is a belief element at the ultimate reaches of the scientific experience. Gravitation, for instance, is both an experience and in some manner a belief, because it is a mystery that we cannot deal with adequately. The ultimates of science are trans-scientific. This type of experience we are having is unique. Reconstituting this within a religious perspective and relating this to a new, larger, more expansive dimension of Christianity is the theological role of our time.

It is something like the situation in the early stages of Christianity and the Christian meeting with the Greek world of thought. The early Greek fathers of the church were confronted with a world of knowledge quite different from the biblical revelatory experience. They had to deal with it, so they worked out the beginnings of what we call theology. The Bible has a theological aspect but is not, strictly speaking, a structured theology. We began to have a structured theology only after contact with the Greek world. Christianity as it exists has been profoundly enriched and has grown precisely because of its contact with an outer world. This enabled Christianity to expand its understanding of itself, also of the divine, and of the processes whereby the human fulfilled its divinely appointed purposes. A little later, Augustine (354-430) gave further development to theology through his contact with the Neoplatonism of his time. In the thirteenth century, St. Thomas Aquinas (1225-1274) entered into the world of Aristotle (384-322 B.C.) and so brought about a new and finely wrought theological expression of Christianity.

The Issues

Religion and Theology

Our world is the world we know through scientific observation, a much different world from the classical world into which Christians first emerged. In both cases, there is continuity and discontinuity. Today, however, we are experiencing a discontinuity unequaled in its order of magnitude. That is why there is such difficulty throughout all the religions of the present time and why we are experiencing new fundamentalisms. We are living now in a world of fundamentalisms: Islamic, Jewish, Christian, Buddhist, Hindu, Shinto. Fundamentalism is a defensive tactic. None of the religions feel equipped to deal with this new challenge. It is why the religions of the world are not dealing with the ecology issue. If we depended on the religions of the world to deal with the ecology issue, we would already be much worse off than we are at present. None of the religions, in my acquaintance, have shown any effective responsibility for the fate of the earth. By not accepting a responsibility for the fate of the earth, there is a failure of religious responsibility to the divine, as well as to the human. We seem not to realize that as the outer world becomes damaged, our sense of the divine is degraded in a corresponding manner.

Why do we have such a wonderful idea of God? Because we live in such a gorgeous world. We wonder at the magnificence of whatever it is that brought the world into being. This leads to a sense of adoration. We have a sense of immense gratitude that we participate in such a beautiful world. This adoration, this gratitude, we call religion. Now, however, as the outer world is diminished, our inner world is dried up.

If we lived on the moon, for example, our sense of the divine would reflect the lunar landscape. We would not have anything like the awareness of the divine that we have at present. Imagination is required for religious development. What would there be to imagine if we lived on the moon? We would have something, but it would be very meagre. Our sensitivities would be dull because our inner world would reflect the outer world. Intelligence would be so stunted that it would be hardly developed at all. Why? Because there would be very little to name, very little to discuss or to talk about. There would still be the great question of existence and nonexistence, so perhaps human intelligence would have some development. We would have some inner life. But think of being born on the moon and then coming to the earth. What a stunning, beatific experience that would be!

In reverse, if we lived on the earth and then put ourselves back on the moon, what would we be missing? We would be moving from a sense of existence, a sense of the human, a sense of the beauty in a creative world, and a sense of the power that brought this into being, back to an extinction of everything that we have here. For religion not to realize that, not to safeguard the basis of its own survival, for humans not to appreciate the source of their arts, their science, their dance, their whole intellectual and affective life, their whole expansiveness of soul and mind and heart, and not to feel that endangered by what we are doing to ourselves: how strange!

God and the Time-Developmental Universe

There are five basic subjects that have been selected for consideration in this unit: God, the Trinity, the role of the human, creation, and revelation. In a certain sense, these all come together: the sense of God, of the human, of creation, and revelation. We cannot deal with these separately. We would have no sense of the divine without creation. Speculatively, we could talk about God as being prior to or outside creation or independent of creation, but in actual fact there is no such being as God without creation. When a person associates the creation with the divine, it is the existential fact that there is no God without creation and there is no creation without God.

As a note here, I would like to mention something that comes up constantly. I do not generally use the word "God" because I think the word has been overused. It is used in so many different ways that it carries too much ambivalence. Also, I wish to address myself to people of any belief, so I try to use words that make sense to everybody. In my writings generally, I am concerned primarily with the larger society, not simply with Christians or even "religious" people.

The term "God" refers to the ultimate mystery of things, something beyond that which we can understand adequately. It is experienced as the Great Spirit by many of the Primal Peoples of the world. The Great Spirit is the all-pervasive, mysterious power that is present and observed in the rising and the setting of the sun, in the growing of living things, in the sequence of the seasons. This mysterious power carries things through to their brilliant expression in all the forms that we observe in the world about us, in the stars at night, in the feel and experience of the wind, in the surging expanse of the oceans. Peoples generally experience an awesome, stupendous presence that cannot be expressed adequately in human words. Since it cannot be expressed in language, people often dance this experience, they express it in music, in art, in the pervasive of the beautiful throughout the whole of daily life, in the laughter of children, in the taste of bread, in the sweetness of an apple. At every moment we are experiencing the overwhelming mystery of existence. It is that simple but that ineffable. What is the divine? It is the ineffable, pervasive presence in the world about us.

One of the things that we have to recognize is that this divine presence in creation is understood differently in our new historical context. Originally, the divine was perceived as manifested throughout the world, throughout the total range of natural phenomena; it was simply a given. There was a spatial experience of the divine manifestation in the natural world. That is, time moved in ever-renewing, seasonal cycles of change. It was eternal. The universe existed as it always was and always would be.

In the biblical world, however, a new sense of history came into being, an awareness that the universe emerged into being at a definite moment. Before that, human consciousness awakened to the universe as the universe always was, always would be, in ever-renewing cycles. Humans could not really interfere with that or change it. They could not begin it, nor could they end it.

Now we have something different in our experience of the universe. We perceive the universe through a new mode of intellectual perception. Earlier, what was involved was immediate intuitive experience: we simply observed the natural world about us. More recently, however, we have begun to look at the natural world in terms of empirical science with the aid of microscopic and telescopic instruments. We have looked at the universe very intensely, studying the stars, for example, trying to find out how they came into being. We have looked at the world about us and have analyzed the elements until we see how things grow. Gradually, we have come to understand that the universe is not simply a given, and that it did indeed have a beginning in time. Time, we discover, is irreversible. The sequence in the larger arc of its development has been from lesser to greater complexity and consciousness.

Our modern scientific view of the universe thus coincides with the biblical realm rather than the non-biblical world, which does not have such a clear sense of an emergent universe which began at a definitive historical moment. As we count back into the ages, we discover that our universe has existed for a vast period of time. Presently we can calculate something like 15 billion years. This understanding of the universe, however, is different from many previous understandings. It is historical, rather than metaphysical, time. In India, for example, the universe (as traditionally understood) comes into being over some trillions of years, to exist for trillions of years, and then is extinguished, only to come back again and again. This view represents a kind of metaphysical time, and is not based on an empirical study of the material cosmos and its history.

The Chinese, on the other hand, have what I would call chronological time in human history. They can tell better than any other people of the world what happened in their history 3000 years ago. They know with a great deal of precision just what was happening then. This I describe as chronological history. Meaningful history, that is, the story of meaningful developmental time, comes into being with the revelatory experience in the Middle East, which was developed in the biblical world and the Christian world. Even with Christians, the universe itself was viewed in an ever-continuing, seasonal time perspective—although the very essence of Christianity is developmental *human* time, the working out of a divine presence in the human world in terms of the kingdom of God. What we have now, through our modern story of the universe, is a new sense of a universe, one that had a precise beginning and has gone through a sequence of differentiating transformations leading from lesser to greater complexity and greater modes of consciousness. These two need, in some manner, to be related, an ascending universe of consciousness and the rise of spiritual community. The universe itself is the most basic expression of community. The universe is the ultimate sacred community.

The beginning of the universe, we now see, was not a homogeneous smudge, but, rather, involved articulated energy constellations bound together in an inseparable unity. The various parts of the universe are outwardly differentiated, inwardly articulated, and bonded together in a comprehensive intimacy of every particle with every other particle. There is something very important about the beginning of the universe as we now know it. I consider this revelatory in a magnificent way, because it tells us something about the powers that brought the universe into being at the beginning.

Let me try to explain. In the beginning, we have this expansive force, a differentiating force. We have the articulated entities that come into being and this takes place shortly after the primordial radiation. Immediately, gravitation comes into being and things are pulled together in a profound intimacy. So we have two forces at the beginning of the universe. We have the emergent diversification process, a kind of explosion process, and then we have a containing process. The attraction that everything has for everything else is most important. Nobody knows what this attraction is. Isaac Newton (1642-1727), who wrote the laws of gravitation, said he did not know what it was at all. He gave the laws for this attraction but he did not know what it was, and nobody to this day can tell you what gravitation is. But we do know that this attractive force and this explosive force constitute what is called the curvature of the universe. Everything that exists comes into existence within this context, the curvature of space. If this rate of emergence had been a trillionth of a fraction faster or a trillionth of a fraction slower, the universe would have either exploded or collapsed. It had to be precise to the trillion trillionth of a margin. Why? Because this curvature of the universe had to be such that the universe could continue expanding and yet neither explode nor collapse. So we have a universe held together, but not held so tightly that its expansion or its creativity would be stifled. If the attraction overcame the expansion, it would collapse. But if the expansion overcame the attraction, then it would explode.

I call this curvature of space "the compassionate curve" of the universe, or the compassionate curve that *embraces* the universe. What do we do when we meet one another? We reach out and embrace one another. That embrace reflects the curvature of the universe. We talk about reflexive thinking on the part of the human mind because we are that being in whom the universe reflects on itself. What is that reflection? That is the expression in human intelligence of the curvature of the universe. It is the curvature of the universe coming back upon itself. There would be no human reflection if it were not for that curvature. There would be no human affection without gravitational attraction. Gravitation, built into this process, binds everything together so closely that nothing can ever be separated from anything else. Alienation is an impossibility, a cosmological impossibility. We can *feel* alienated, but we can never *be* alienated.

The other thing that is so important in this process is the relationship of origin. Everything in the universe is genetically cousin to everything else. There is literally one family, one bonding, in the universe, because everything is descended from the same source. In this creative process, all things come into being. On the planet earth, all living things are clearly derived from a single origin. We are literally born as a community; the trees, the birds, and all living creatures are bonded together in a single community of life. This again gives us a sense that we belong. Community is not something that we dream up or think would be nice. Literally, we are a single community. The planet earth is a single community of existence, and we exist in this context.

The Trinity

One of the remarkable things about Christian belief is that it goes beyond the question of the divine as the only being that is pure simplicity, a pure flame of existence. All other beings are "put-together" beings. Only the divine is a not-put-together being. This is generally true of the different religions. Simplicity is a metaphysical definition of the divine. There exists in the Christian world, however, this sense that the inner life of the divine is community. To say that community is at the heart of the ultimate simplicity is a challenging statement!

We first have this expressed in the Bible in terms of what is called the family model, the Father, Son and Spirit: the Father, the emergent principle; the Son, the inner articulation of things; and the Holy Spirit, the bonding force of things. We then have St. Augustine, who explains the Trinity with a psychological model: thought thinking itself, which is considered something of the inner life of pure spirit, that self-awareness and self-bonding that takes place within the depths of this ultimate reality. In modern times, we have what is known as the sociological model of Trinity: the self, the other, and the community. But I propose that there is a new and in some ways better model based on cosmology and the functioning of the universe. That is the model of differentiation, inner articulation, and communion, which emerges from our scientific understanding of the universe.

We experience the world as emergent diversification and differentiation; each particle has its own interiority. Every particle has its identifying inner structure, its inner being. In a sense, everything participates "in person," as it were, everything has its voice. Everything speaks itself and everything is receiving something from every other particle of the universe. So we get the communion of things. The volume of each atom is the volume of the universe (if you consider that every atom is where its influence is being felt). Every atom is immediately influencing every other atom in the universe, no matter how distant, even if it is billions of billions of light years away. There is still the bonding. So the explanation of Trinity in our times, in light of the cosmological model, would be in terms of a principle of differentiation: the Father; the principle of interior articulation, the inner principle of things: the Son; and the Holy Spirit, the bonding, the holding together of things, the spirit of love, the *spiritus*, the inner spirit of reality.

The Primary Sacred Community

I consider that our new understanding of the universe is a new revelatory experience. It is not revelation in the sense that the Bible is revelation, but it is nevertheless revelatory. It is the way in which the divine is presently revealing itself to us. We do not read this even in the Psalms. (We can get wonderful insights from the Psalms; they are a very precious presentation of the way in which the entire natural world sings the divine praise.) We now have a new insight into the sacred community, and that is why I say the universe itself is the primary sacred community. It is the primary religious reality. It is the primary governance of the universe. It is the primary everything. And we exist as distinctive members of this universe.

This revelation is not proceeding by the same process as traditional revelation has proceeded. In other words, this procedure we are going through, using rational, analytic processes, is entirely different from those intuitive processes that the prophets experienced. It is a different modality. It also results in a different sense of how the divine, the ultimate mystery of things, presents itself to us. This experience is as unique as is the revelatory experience of the Hindu world. This too is qualitatively different from the revelatory experience of the biblical world. What is it that gives these experiences the capacity to be called revelation? It is the practical mode in which the divine is communicated and how the divine and human are communicating with each other. That is the larger dimension of the revelatory category, but it functions in different ways. Flowers are flowers but there is a qualitative difference among flowers. Trees are trees but there is no such thing as "a tree" that is not a specific kind of tree, an individual expression of its species.

Behind all of this, I think, is something often said about "the scandal of particular election" in Christian theology. It is the divine election of a chosen people, of a chosen, unique revelation. Rather than the *scandal* of particularity, I think of it as the *absurdity* of particularity, because the universe is an integral community. The universe has this singular reality. The universe has to be the *primary* election. As St. Thomas Aquinas (1224?-1274) says in Part One, Question 47, Article One, of the *Summa Theologica,* the reason there are so many different things in the world is because God cannot create another deity. God cannot communicate God's self totally to any one being, and so creates this array of beings so that the perfection lacking in one would be supplied by the other, and the total universe of things would manifest and participate in the divine more than any single being. The primary election, the primary concern, has to be the totality, and anything that is elected has to be chosen in light of the totality. It is not to do away with differentiation, because differentiation is the grandeur of the totality of things. Within this primary election, *everything* is elected, each in its own modality.

Interestingly, in the Hindu world, the same thing is experienced. Hindus experience themselves as an elected, unique mode of presence to the divine, a unique mode of being. The Buddhists, too, have a unique spiritual communication. In other words, everything is elected in its own very special way, but everything is also elected in the sense of a unique communication. The Hindu and Buddhist traditions have their own particularity and universality. Anyone who does not benefit from these other traditions is, I think, lacking something.

17

I was once with a group of people, and there was a woman philosopher there. I was talking about my Buddhist soul and my Hindu soul and my Chinese soul. I could see that she was getting more and more tense. Pretty soon she pounded the table and said, "What do you believe?" And I said, "I believe everything. Tell me something, I'll believe it. I am a believer and I like to believe. Why should I limit my belief?" As St. Paul says, "Believe all things." The norm for my belief is really the earth community norm, that is, how the human has responded to the conditions of life over the centuries, in different cultures and at different times. For instance, take a very simple thing like spiritual rebirth ceremonies. I have never discovered a people who does not have spiritual rebirth ceremonies. When we come across something so constant, we know there is something very profound and prevalent, a need of the human psyche, a common feature of human spiritual formation. There is a specific Christian manifestation of it, but, in itself, it has much broader significance.

We really have a "multiverse" as well as a universe, where everything is differentiated but everything and everybody is elected; in every election, there is universal election as well as particular election. The devastation of the planet is attributable to this exaggerated understanding of particularity in election in the biblical, Western tradition. In this case, it is the feeling that only the human—and not the natural world—is elected. This neglect of the natural world cannot endure. There can be no adequate sacred community without the inclusion of the natural world.

Traditional Ideas of a Transcendent God

The divine is experienced by peoples generally as an all-pervasive presence of mysterious power in the universe. We biblical people have drawn all this pervasive presence together and constellated it in a transcendent, divine, personal creator related by covenant to a special people. Well, by doing this, what do we gain and what do we lose? We do gain something. I would describe the first pages of the Bible as the triumph of the heaven-father over the earth-mother. The First Commandment is "Thou shall not have an earth mother."

I do not mind a heaven father, that is all right. But I do like the idea of an earth mother, and I also like to talk to the trees. This idea that the trees talk to me and I talk to the trees, this kind of subjectivity, is somehow absent from our tradition. People say it is in the Psalms and here and there, and it is in the tradition somewhere. But traditions are their historical reality. You cannot say there is an "ideal Christianity" somewhere out there. When I talk about Christianity, I talk about the historical reality of Christianity. The historical reality is that Christians, like St. Boniface (680?–755, the English missionary to Germany), cut down the oak trees deemed sacred by pagans.

Why were the pagans seen as idolatrous? The divine always appears in some embodiment; no one ever worshiped matter as matter. Whatever is worshiped is seen as a mode of divine presence. There is a wonderful passage in the most sacred text of the Hindu world. I think it is one of the most beautiful and relevant passages in religious writings anyway. It is a work called the *Bhagavad Gita*, the Song of the Lord. One of the passages says, "Wherever anyone worships me, I make my presence felt there." Why should not the divine make its presence where people locate the divine? Intuitively, we know that the divine goodness does that. The divine obviously is there or nothing would exist. St. Augustine says that God is more intimate to us than we are to ourselves. God is more intimate to everything. Every existence is a mode of divine presence. There is indeed a difference, a distinction, but if there were a difference in the sense of separation, the created world would not be. I could not exist except for a divine presence. There is always the mystery of things, and the mystery of existence can be given the name divine, it can be called God or immanence or whatever one wishes. We must admit the mystery of things. Few persons ever thought that they really could exhaustively resolve the mystery of anything. I do not perceive a great problem with this immanence and transcendence issue. It does seem, however, that our excessive emphasis on transcendence is leading us to destroy the planet.

Today, we have a wonderful resource in the indigenous peoples of the world who now are assuming a leadership role in human affairs. This is after a large number of other peoples have taken possession of the earth and have been more in command of what happens to the planet. As soon as we get into the ecological issues, we begin to learn from these indigenous peoples. We have something like 200 million indigenous peoples of the world, also referred to as First Peoples or Primal Peoples.

One of the first things that we learn from these peoples is that the universe is a community of subjects, not a collection of objects. We have been treating the universe as a collection of objects. No matter how much these are interrelated with each other, if we do not hear the voices of the trees, the birds, the animals, the fish, the mountains and the rivers, then we are in trouble. I think that is one of the most important things that we are learning from the tribal peoples of the world. We are learning to address the river and be addressed by the river.

Not long ago, I was talking with several hundred high school students at one of the prestigious high schools in the city of New York. I said that my generation has been an autistic generation. I asked them what autism was. Imagine asking a group of high school students what "autism" is! One student got up and explained very clearly: persons being so locked up in themselves that no one and nothing else can get in. It is an isolation process. That, I think, is what has happened to the human community in our times. We are talking to ourselves. We are not talking to the river, we are not listening to the river. We have broken the great conversation. By breaking the conversation, we have shattered the universe. All these things that are happening now are consequences of this autism. As we become more and more aware of the tragic destiny that we are now caught in, we are driven more and more back to Primal Peoples' experience. In this regard, I think the communications given us by Black Elk are particularly important, especially in *Black Elk Speaks* (John Neihardt, New York: Washington Square Press, 1972. Original edition, 1921).

Through Black Elk, we can relearn how to listen. There are many other things, of course, that we can learn from Primal Peoples, but this I would suggest is one thing of immense importance that we are learning from them.

Related to this is the enormously important question of animism. I often suggest that the salvation of Christians lies in the unassimilated elements of paganism. We have assimilated the Greek wisdom. We are assimilating the Oriental mystique, as well as the meditation techniques of different parts of the world. We have assimilated much of what China has to offer. Why, then, do we exclude the assimilation of the culture of "pagan people"? It is another instance of a difficulty during these past centuries when we isolated ourselves. We felt threatened somehow. We withdrew. That might be historically understandable, but its continuation cannot be accepted. It is like, as I mentioned, St. Boniface cutting down the sacred oak trees. Today that would be absurd. The unassimilated elements of paganism have so much to offer us in establishing an intimate rapport with the natural world.

The Role of the Human Species

When we talk about the creation of the human, what exactly do we mean by "human"? The human is that being in whom the universe reflects on and celebrates itself and its numinous origin in its own, unique mode of conscious self-awareness. All living beings do this in their own way, but in the human, this becomes a dominant mode of functioning. It is not that we think on the universe; the universe, rather, thinks *itself*, in us and through us. This is a more wonderful definition of the human than is the classical definition, which identifies humans as rational animals. This is a good biological definition. But there is another way of looking at the human. For instance, the Chinese have always identified the human as the *hsin* of the universe. *Hsin* is their word for the heart. Written as a pictograph of a human heart, it is translated in this context as "mind" and also as "heart" of the universe. For the Chinese, the human is the "mind and heart of the universe."

This brings me to an observation which I think is most important in talking about the human. There are always two modes of any being, its microphase mode and its macrophase mode, in other words, its particular mode and its universal mode. We are not ourselves without everything else. We have many selves: our personal self, our family self, and our community self. We are never really apart from ourselves. When we say, "I do things not for myself but for my family," it is not entirely true. We do things for our family self as well as our personal self because these are identified. We exist for our human self, our community self, our earth self, and our universe self.

In this sense, we are not simply genetically cousin to everything else but we have a certain identity with everything else. We cannot save ourselves without saving everything and everybody else. Unless we are activated by some other person, we cannot be our true selves. We depend on each other to give us ourselves. We become a self by giving ourselves and receiving ourselves. We exist in this comprehensive context. If we lose the outer world, we lose the inner world. Always we are being drawn back to our larger self. Why am I drawn to a person? There is where "I am." There is where I exist. A person says, "You are everything." It is entirely true. The other person is everything, but a person also must have an inner self-articulation to be able to experience this, to experience the self in the other, the self in the community, the self in the universe. Because we are so intimate with the earth, if we degrade the planet, we degrade our larger self. It is suicide.

Many people inquire about the level of animal intelligence, and how it compares to human. We have to recognize that intelligence exists in vastly different modalities. It is best not to speak of "levels," but simply to speak of qualitative differences. Intelligence is highly diversified in its expression and in its functioning. The differences are qualitative, not quantitative. In qualitative differences there is not exactly higher or lower but the modality of their functioning. Each has its higher development in relation to its proper functioning. So in the world of the honey bee, the peregrine falcon, the rainbow trout, the dolphin, and the human—in each case the intelligence is appropriate to its function; each is perfect in its own order. The special mode of human intelligence lies in the high development of its reflexive consciousness. These various forms of intelligence in their natural state are all present to each other in a profound understanding and sympathetic relationship. The splendid aspect of this presence lies precisely in the differences. Because each is unique they can enhance each other, introducing each other into areas of experience that could not exist if the differences were less extensive. Each carries the deep mysteries of existence in some special mode of expression. Among humans, poets are most profoundly in communion with these other modes of understanding. Yet in childhood we often experience this communion with those other forms. Our autism is the result of our education.

Science and Teilhard de Chardin

The work of French Jesuit paleontologist Pierre Teilhard de Chardin often comes up in such discussions concerning the relationship of the human to the created world. There is good reason for this. Teilhard de Chardin, around 1940, wrote the basic work of twentieth-century theology. It was never taken up, although it remains, possibly, the most powerful restatement of theology since the time of St. Paul.

In his work, Teilhard showed that the Christian story was identical to the universe story and that if we could only understand it in this light, then theological studies would become more integral. They would become more powerful. They would be able to deal effectively with the distraught human community and with the ecological upset. They would assist considerably in healing our human relationship with the divine. From now on, there is going to be, in my estimation, no effective human relationship with the divine that is not integral with this story of the universe that we know at the present time. If we can renew theology, renew our religious relationship with the universe, then we can assist more effectively in healing the psychic difficulties of people who cannot deal adequately with life because they do not see meaning in things. A new ecological spirituality will emerge. We will attain our religious well-being, our human well-being, and our planetary well-being.

Teilhard had three basic achievements. He was the first person to describe the universe as having, from the beginning, a psychic-spiritual dimension as well as a physical-material dimension. Secondly, he identified the human story with the universe story. Science now is well aware that the human is integral with the story of the universe, and they are now asking about the relationship between the mind that the universe produces, and the mind that knows the universe. Presently, scientists speak of the "cosmological anthropic principle," an extremely significant principle, involving the inner structuring and functioning of the universe in its microphase dimensions. Freeman Dyson, a professor of physics at Princeton University, says that the more he studies the structure of the universe, the clearer it is to him that the universe must have known from the beginning that we were coming. This is in accord with all the elements of chance and natural selection that go into shaping the universe as it now is. Ultimately there is, in the universe, a direction toward "complexity-centration," as Teilhard says.

Thirdly, Teilhard stressed the importance of moving from excessive concern for the redemption process to a greater emphasis on the creation process. As early as 1931, he wrote quite clearly of "the self-organizing dimension of the universe."

This self-organizing dimension of the universe does not mean that there is not a deeper mystery in the origin of this power within the universe. In other words, it excludes neither the further mystery of how this self-organizing dimension is communicated, nor how it functions, because in the phenomenal world, the universe is the only self-referent reality. We can never know the universe in any adequate way because we have nothing to compare it to, nothing to relate it to—it is the only self-referential reality in the phenomenal world. It is the only text without context. Everything else has to be seen in the context of the universe. This is why our sense of creation is so distinct, and why the fundamentalists will not accept the fact that the universe is self-creation within the divine context. A person can talk about a context in the order of mystery or transcendence, or the numinous context of the universe, which could be considered the divine dimension. But God is not constantly running the show as though the universe were made up of puppets. It is not a puppet show, it is a reality, functioning from within its own spontaneity.

It is so remarkable and so stupendous to come to understand this process. The divine enables the universe to function in this remarkable way. There is a capacity of self-articulation inherent in the universe, and the more we know about that, the more clear it is that we will gain a totally different sense of the universe than we had previously, and a different sense of how the divine functions in relation to the universe.

I do, however, have some criticisms of Teilhard. It is somewhat tragic that he is not fully "available" for contemporary ecologists because he was so intensely committed to the technological world. For Teilhard, totally the evolutionary process was concentrated in the human. He could not understand the devastating aspect of the human. When Henry Fairfield Osborne in his 1947 book, *Our Plundered Planet,* proposed that, through human deeds, the world was undergoing grave ecological devastation, Teilhard refused to accept that this was happening. Others could see it, but Teilhard could not. He had an excessive optimism, based, I believe, on Jean de Caussade's *Abandonment to Divine Providence* (1861), a work of French spirituality. De Caussade encouraged abandonment to God's will. During World War I, Teilhard had a sense of excitement about being at the front. For him the worse things were, the better, because it meant that God had even more grand plans for things. Teilhard could not take seriously the destruction of the natural world. Once, when someone pointed out to him the destruction of the natural world, Teilhard said that science would discover other forms of life.

I would like to situate theology in terms of understanding the meaning of science.

Science itself is ultimately a mythic form of understanding. Physicist Wolfgang Pauli (1900–1958), for example, attributed his discoveries to archetypal dream experiences. Sir Isaac Newton (1642–1727), the archetypal scientist, was not, interestingly enough, a mechanist. Later, people interpreted him as a mechanist, but he was, in reality, more an alchemist. He spent most of his life studying the mysteries of things and trying to get into them through alchemy. He candidly acknowledged that he did not know what gravitation was. It was too deep a mystery for him. It was taking him into the world of mystery.

With contemporary science, and our new sense of things (since quantum physics and Werner Heisenberg [1901–1976]), we get far beyond mechanism. There are mechanistic scientists but the reflective scientists in a larger context are aware of the deeper mysteries of existence. It is like Heisenberg's "uncertainty principle": our contact with things changes things. We do not really know things in themselves in their objective reality, but rather by an intercommunion.

Every scientific formula is as much myth and mystery as it is rational understanding. What is it that unifies the formula? The formula is nothing without its interpretation, so the understanding is not in the formula. (No formula is self-interpreting.) Scientists think it is there because they can make the equation work. I am not exactly arguing that the rational scientific process is a dream process, but it functions in the context of an even deeper mystery that many scientists are beginning to recognize. As soon as we admit this, we have a much larger mystery. Our science does not reduce the mystery, it enhances the mystery.

Because Christians could not appreciate our new understanding of the universe, they failed to enter into new modes whereby the divine reveals itself. Christians seek understanding, in some kind of deductive way, solely from their own resources. They have, as a result, not yet been able to accept the scientific vision and see its religious value. There is enormous religious value in the new story of the universe, but Christian theology still cannot appreciate this story as its own sacred story.

If theology is not itself in a healthy situation, how can theology contribute to healing the larger culture in our present, disturbed situation? Indigenous peoples generally have healing rituals that are cosmologically based. For instance, the Navajo, in healing rituals, tell the story of the universe. They even image the universe in their dry paintings. The person to be healed is placed within the painting. Then the healing process is worked out with the invocation of the powers of the universe in relationship to the particular difficulty that the person is experiencing. So the healing process is always a cosmological community process, the community of the water and the air and the soil and the herbs and the insects. Our medicines come from these sources, from the living forms, from various plants, from insects, and so forth. We need to re-establish a rapport with the universe and its mysterious powers.

The difficulty is that theology, in its fidelity to the past, has isolated itself from the larger community of life and existence in the present. It was not always this way, however, during the great periods of creativity in theology. At the time of the fathers of the church in the early centuries, for instance, it was amazing how effectively Clement of Alexandria (150?-220?) put Christian belief in relationship to the Greek world, the larger human order, and the larger cosmological order in the context of his times. Later, Augustine put the theology of the church in relationship to the Neoplatonism of his period. Augustine, in a sense, created the Middle Ages, largely through his work *The City of God*. It is the story of the universe and the story of the human in the universe. It was in the context of this story that medieval Christendom was born.

In the time of St. Thomas, there was a need for a contact and a reinterpretation of the Greek world of metaphysics, mind, and natural law. So, St. Thomas wrote a summation of all theology in his *Summa Theologica*. Through his rapport with the remarkable works of Aristotle, he was able to write this comprehensive interpretation of Christian belief. Later, the church, during the Renaissance, experienced a further elaboration of its teachings.

Theology, in recent times, has lost contact with our present story of the universe. In doing this, it has lost contact with the larger human community. Our traditional story of the universe has become dysfunctional. We have a new story that we have learned through the empirical sciences. The difficulty is that this story has been told as a mechanistic process, as a chance process, as a purely rational process, as something that had no mystique to it, no numinous quality. It had no spirit, so to speak, no "personal" quality. We need to discover this story of an emergent universe—in a time-developmental sequence of transformations—as our sacred story. We have the story. It is not yet accepted as our sacred story.

Because of his awareness of the emergent universe, I consider Teilhard more important to my own thinking than Alfred North Whitehead (1861–1947). Whitehead, unlike Teilhard, did not have a clear idea of realistic, historical time. He was a philosopher-scientist, not an historian or a naturalist or a paleontologist. He understood process time, but he did not have a grasp of an integral history in its phenomenal reality. He understood the universe as an organism, as holistic, as integral, as interacting, as a process, but he did not have it going anywhere. The story is missing in Whitehead. Teilhard had the story. This also is one of the differences between Thomas Merton (1915–1968) and Teilhard. The power of Thomas Merton is in his spiritual vision. The power of Teilhard is in his comprehensive story of the universe as both psychic and material, that is, spirit and physical. Why were Hegel (1770–1831) and Marx (1818–1883) so powerful? They had the story of the emergent process. Without a story, it is difficult to have a comprehensive, sustained influence in our present world.

THOMAS CLARKE

The Context

Thomas Berry and Theology

They say that first sentences are important, so here is my first sentence. Tom Berry is that member of the human species in whom the emerging universe has come to a unique celebratory moment of reflective self awareness.

Tom Berry has not been particularly waiting with baited breath for the following sentence but after spending several months going through some of Tom's works, it occurs to me, as an "orthodox" theologian and one of Teilhard's waverers, that Tom has given us a system which is not only brilliant, but which, at least from my limited perspective, is quite congruous with the Judaeo-Christian heritage which is part of Tom's own background.

Christian Revelation and the New Cosmology

Theology is in a much better position today than it was in 1950 to assimilate some of what Tom is saying about revelation, because we have moved from a cognitive, verbal, supernatural understanding to an idea of divine revelation as co-extensive with creation. Everything speaks of God. This gets differentiated in this emerging order of the universe. From the Christian standpoint, the primary revelation has taken place in Jesus of Nazareth—his life, death, and exaltation—and continues to take place centrally in him, but that does not mean that it is not taking place primarily within the processes of the universe, because human beings *are* the universe come to reflective self-awareness. What happened in and through Jesus of Nazareth and what is happening in the Body of Christ, which we are now being called to extend? It seems to me that the new cosmology can do a tremendous amount for traditional Christian theology: it can heal it. Traditional Christian theology, however, perhaps also can help the new cosmology in a few of the ways that I will indicate.

The Issues

On Naming God

It is always a dangerous thing to talk about God, especially today when theology has to speak to the concreteness of human life, this immense ecological question, as Tom Berry has described it. While discernment is necessary, discernment is not caution. Discernment, I think, involves a great deal of trust and hope. I like to say the favorite word for theology is not "therefore" but "nevertheless," because we have to keep overcoming what we have just said.

I appreciate Tom Berry's reason for not too quickly saying the word "God." I think a too ready recourse to God-language can diminish the reverence and the sense of mystery which is important for us to have in the presence of the divine. Secondly, God-talk can too easily be an escape from human responsibility or can disengage us from that element of the sacred which is present in God's creation. We can too quickly go from created reality to the reality of the creator. So, on that point, I would say that Tom has a good, very plausible case to make for not saying "God" too quickly. That is congruous with the Christian tradition, back to the fathers of the church who used such expressions as, "We know what God is not, rather than what God is," "We know that God is, we do not know how God is," or, as St. Augustine says beautifully in Latin, "*Si comprehendisti, non est Deus.*" If you have really grasped the reality of God, it is not God that you have grasped, because God constantly escapes us. I think what we are struggling for at this juncture is to explore the relationship between the new cosmology and traditional Christian doctrine and Christian theology. We are focusing, from the standpoint of the tradition, on God, creation, revelation, and the Trinity. So let me try to address at least some of these from the vantage point of the tradition.

Creation in the New Revelatory Moment

First of all, this theological notion of creation represents a Judaeo-Christian response to the question, "Why is there anything at all?," a question which science as such does not ask but which we as humans and as religious have to ask. The response of our tradition is that the universe exists because it is a creation of God. There is no time to go into the whole critique of modern philosophy, which claims that the Christian doctrines of creation and providence inhibit human freedom and human autonomy. Modern theologians have tried to work out a response to that critique, a notion of creation and a notion of providence in which God simply transcends our experience of creation on the human level so that, far from our dependence on a creator God inhibiting our freedom, it is a challenge to exercise our freedom. Karl Rahner (1904-1988), for example, said that God, precisely because God is God, is able to constitute another being in existence in a radical dependence upon God. Then, not in spite of but precisely *because* of that, the creature is constituted with a certain autonomy. Tom Berry could testify to the way in which Aquinas, in his understanding of this creator-creature relationship, gave to the creature, and especially to the human creature, a full freedom to exercise its inherent created powers.

This is a statement I am not sure of, but it is perhaps a sign that I have not really assimilated Tom Berry's message fully. Let me throw it out anyway. From the standpoint of this radical notion of creation, of God transcendent, constituting the universe in existence with all of its dynamics having a certain autonomy, the transition from cosmos to cosmogenesis tends to be relativized. Now if I had time, I would add a "nevertheless" to that: I have to be honest and say that I look at this revolutionary transition from that closed cosmos, with which our ancestors had to deal, to this revelation of cosmogenesis, and, from the particular point of view of a Christian who believes in God the creator, at least one side of me says, "How much difference does it make?"

Immanence and Transcendence

My understanding of creation is that creation takes place through a God who, in the traditional language, is both transcendent and immanent. Tom Berry, in his essays, talks about acknowledging the legitimacy of the notion of transcendence, but he mentions the concrete harm that has taken place. This theological or philosophical notion of divine transcendence has done harm, particularly in disengaging us from communion with the earth. It is a difficult thing today to speak a word in behalf of divine transcendence. I would acknowledge that what Tom Berry has described has happened. We could quarrel about the details of it but all of these notions are beneficial and harmful at the same time. But I would want to maintain that, especially to the extent to which we succeed in disengaging this notion of divine transcendence from patriarchy, militarism, and the sense of a non-accountable deity running the universe—to the extent to which we can disengage this notion of divine transcendence from those cultural accoutrements—it seems to me that divine transcendence has a word to speak in our context today.

Basically, I think we could look at divine transcendence from a twofold point of view. First, we could look at it ontologically. What God's transcendence says is that the universe is not God, that when we have the whole reality of the universe, there is still God. From that point of view, it seems to me that what the Judaeo-Christian accent on divine transcendence has done has been to warn us against idolatry. Nothing finite, nothing that is in a univocal sense this universe, is the God whom we worship. I think divine transcendence reminds us of that. Second, we could look at it epistemologically. What divine transcendence says is that we can never capture God. God, the divine in the literal sense, is undefined and is constantly beyond us. So it seems to me that, in this twofold way, God is not the universe and that our knowledge of God never succeeds in catching up with God. There is a role for this understanding of divine transcendence, but if it is to exercise that role, it has to exercise it in tandem, so to speak, with the companion notion of divine immanence. This is what has been to a large extent neglected in our Christian tradition.

Ontologically, divine immanence would say that we are not to conceive of divine transcendence as indicating that God is distinct from the universe, and far off, but that every created reality, every human reality, participates in the reality of God. Divine immanence in the whole of creation, and especially in the human expression of creation, is the ground for that dimension of the sacred which, as Tom Berry continually points out, is part of our experience of the universe, that creative reality which evokes in us that sense of sacredness. Divine immanence, as manifested in the Holy Spirit, grounds a reverent, sacramental approach to the whole of creation. Epistemologically, divine immanence says that even though we can never capture God through our knowledge, every act of human knowledge nevertheless has God present to it, has God as the horizon, so that whether or not we are thinking about God, the reality of God is a dimension of all human knowledge.

The Trinity: A More Immanent Sense

In terms of the trinitarian aspect of God, there are so many different models that we can use. Tom Berry presented an attractive cosmological model. I would like to take the trinitarian mystery and relate it to creation in terms of transcendence and immanence.

I would say that the one who is called God in the New Testament, God the Father, stands for God as transcendent, God as hidden, as silent, as in some fashion absent, God whose face we do not see. It is in the Face, in the Word, that we come to whatever dark knowledge of God we are capable of in this life. And this Word is spoken, not just in Judaeo-Christian revelation, but in the whole universe and in each of the creatures. I would accent the ongoing character of creation in this view. Every human experience, as Tom Berry has been pointing out, is revelation, and God's Word is constantly being spoken to us, no matter what we are doing. The Spirit appears as God immanent in the whole of creation.

God is Spirit, breathing forth. The Word is spoken, the Spirit is breathed, and that Spirit becomes the life of our life, the soul of our soul. That would be a brief description of how this notion of creation with God transcendent and immanent could be reflected in our trinitarian statements.

The Universe and Self-Reflection

I would like to respond to the issue about other species and reflectiveness. I had read quite a few of Tom Berry's essays before I came to his acknowledgment of a certain notion and when I came to that, I heaved a huge sigh of relief. It was the notion of analogy and I was brought up on the analogy of being. In such statements as those concerning the attribution of consciousness and a certain psychic life to all the beings of the universe—when Tom Berry indicates that we have that in common with all other beings—the traditional in me agrees, but analogously; we are not using this language in the same sense. I think you could still have an argument, because a lot of philosophers still would not accept the attribution of consciousness below the plant world to rocks, to what we used to call "the inanimate world." There would still be a quarrel on that. As a theologian, not as a philosopher, I grant the legitimacy of this extension of the ideas of consciousness and psychic life to all the beings of the universe, but it is analogous predication, an analogous statement.

From what Tom Berry has said about us as that species in which the universe thinks itself, the question in my mind is, "Does the universe have a self-reflective mind?" I see only two self-reflective minds. One is the properly divine mind of God, and the other is the human mind. So this new language, which states—instead of thinking of ourselves as in a sense containing the universe—that the universe has thought us, makes me uncomfortable. I see God as thinking the whole universe and thinking of it as cosmogenesis, but it is only when we come to the human that we have a creature of God which shares with God not just consciousness or psychic life, but also the power of reflective consciousness.

Theology as Story

I would fully agree with Tom Berry that the theology which had lost touch with the story became sick, and getting back in touch with the new story is a way back to health. In the last decade or so, theology as story has become a major theme among theologians; I think that is a sign of hope. Theology is faith in search of understanding and faith responds to revelation. For too long it was the cognitive dimension of revelation and faith which too exclusively preoccupied theologians. What has been happening in the last few decades is that our understanding of faith and revelation has been broadening, and now we understand that behind doctrine, behind the cognitive statements which theologians make, there is myth, there is story. So I think that a continuation of that process is what has to happen.

Secondly, I would say theology, at least in the Roman Catholic church, has become sick because it has not been sufficiently open to God's revelation as it emerges from the grassroots of the church, through the people of God. When we hear the word theology, I suspect that most of us still think of the *magisterium* and professional theologians. One of the reasons why we have those recurrent quarrels between the magisterium and professional theologians—witness the most recent document from the Congregation for the Doctrine of the Faith on how theologians are to behave—is that there is a missing partner in that dialogue. It has not been a full dialogue. Only when the grassroots of the church—the laity of the church—have a chance to tell their story and reflect on it, empowered by their baptism and confirmation, not by any kind of special certification, will theology begin to recover. When the story comes from the lips of the entire people of God, theology will be back on the road toward greater health.

Christian Animism

Tom Berry spoke about our need to listen to the experience of native peoples. How, as Christian theologians, can we learn to listen to the people of the native religions? I think a place for us to begin is with the theology of the Holy Spirit. We must begin to accent our theology with a great emphasis on the Holy Spirit as immanent, not just in baptized Christians, but in all peoples and the whole of creation. I have been saying to myself recently that what is needed today is a Christian animism; in the past it was a threat for Christians, which Tom Berry has elaborated in his cultural and historical analysis. It was a threat to Christian theologies wedded to the Word coming to us from the transcendent God. When that theology came into contact with these other "pagan religions," we felt threatened, and thought that this meant that the worship of the one true God was jeopardized if we opened ourselves to the many deities which we perceived in these different religions. I think we are in a new period. I think the more firm we are in our own faith in the one God, the more open we can be to believing that God can be manifest in many, many different ways and is manifest through the processes of the earth, and it is to this that the native religions have been most attuned.

QUESTIONS FOR REFLECTION AND DISCUSSION

1. Thomas Berry claims that we have come to the end of the Cenozoic era and are entering an "Ecozoic" period. Why do you think Berry makes this claim?

2. What is unique about the present revelatory moment, in Berry's view? Do you also regard this moment as unique?

3. Would you disagree, or agree, with Thomas Clarke's assessment that Berry's system "is quite congruous with the Judaeo-Christian heritage"? Why or why not?

4. Would you assess Berry's emphasis on the present scientific understanding of the universe as the key to a vital religious future dangerous or hopeful? Why?

5. For what reasons do you think Thomas Berry considers Teil-

hard de Chardin the most important theologian since St. Paul? Do you agree with this claim?

6. In what ways do you think "story" is used by Berry and Clarke as the important element in revitalizing theology today?

7. Clarke mentions an over-emphasis on transcendence in the Christian tradition. How does he think this emphasis might be balanced?

8. What do you think we can learn from the First Nations of the planet?

9. Berry suggests that "our science does not reduce the mystery, it enhances the mystery." To what extent do you agree or disagree?

CHAPTER TWO

Sacred Community, Spiritual Discipline, and Ritual

IN THIS CHAPTER, Berry emphasizes a new sense of spiritual discipline to which we are called as we move into the Ecozoic period. While citing several requirements for moving to the Ecozoic age, Berry identifies the primary one as a move from anthropocentrism to "biocentrism," and, by extension, "geocentrism." Biocentrism, for Berry, means a sense of community with the whole earth, rather than a sense of community simply with other persons. His use of the exodus motif in this regard is rich in implications, suggesting that we have been either slaves in a foreign land, or lost in a desert of our own making. He offers the provocative pronouncement, "The human community and the natural world will go into the future as a single sacred community or we will both perish in the desert."

Berry critiques our present day religious education, rituals, and sacraments for ignoring the natural world. This point seems hard for many theologians to accept. Berry's primary claim is that, while there are strands in the tradition that deal well with the natural world, these elements are not emphasized in Christian catechesis, liturgy, or preaching. Content analysis would certainly bear him out.

Berry also elucidates what he calls the "shadow side" of the Western tradition: a certain fascination with tragedy, which he links to our inability to stop our present pathologically destructive path. He indicates that we must feel our peril, not so we are paralyzed, but so that we will get on with the enormous task of a new exodus.

Lastly, he outlines the relationship between ecology and Third World issues, arguing that by ignoring the health of eco-systems, we will only increase the difficulties of the poor.

In his response, Thomas Clarke emphasizes that Berry's formulation of one sacred community is a new idea, a key insight to which the church must listen. Clarke develops his understanding on the basis of analogy, yet still argues for a new respect for the community of the universe. He then questions whether the rejection of the concept of stewardship—a notion sometimes suggested to help us overcome our separation from the natural world—is a wise development.

Clarke also outlines the link between liberation theology, with its option for the poor, and the wider community of creatures that we have oppressed. Recalling the biblical parable of the rich man, Dives, and the poor beggar, Lazarus, he calls the human species "Dives" in relation to other species.

THOMAS BERRY

The Context

Spiritual Discipline in a Time of Exodus

As we discuss spiritual discipline, sacred community, and ritual, I would like to begin with the central symbol of the Bible, the symbol of exodus. This is the overarching symbol of the biblical world and the overarching symbol of Western civilization. We ourselves are in transition. We are now at the terminal phase of the Cenozoic, the period that gave special brilliance to the biosystems of the natural world as we have it. This is the setting in which humans came into existence. We have not been here many years. There have been hominid types for several million years, but the immediate ancestors of present humans appeared about 100,000 years ago. They existed for the major part of that 100,000 years in what is known as the Paleolithic period. The development of villages and the domestication of plants and animals came some 12,000 years ago. The classical civilizations as we know them emerged in the past 5000 years. But in the past several hundred years, particularly in the twentieth century, we have mortally wounded many of the life systems of the planet earth. We are in a terminal phase of the Cenozoic period. The tropical rain forests that came into existence in this period are in the process of being extinguished at the rate of more than an acre a second. They are among the most beautiful expressions of life on the planet, among the most beautiful things in all of creation.

I recently saw a series of paintings of tropical flowers that were done by Margaret Mee, an artist who went to the Amazon region when she was about forty years old (See *In Search of Flowers of the Amazon Forest,* ed. Tony Morrison; London: Nonesuch Publications, 1988). During her seven journeys there, she painted the Amazon flowers, which exhibit such exotic beauty and splendor and awesomeness. I was going through that book and the beauty of the flowers that exist there—nowhere else—was just staggering. Yet these are part of the rain forests that are being extinguished at a disastrous rate. This causes a person to think, "What are we looking for in life? Are we looking for beauty or joy or excitement? Are we looking for poetry? Are we looking for understanding? Are we looking for the divine? What are we looking for?" Why would we extinguish, in such a ruthless and senseless manner, something so beautiful as the quintessence of magnificence, the quintessence of life, the quintessence of grandeur? This is what we are doing at the present time. We are also, of course, diminishing the ozone layer at the same time and putting our poisons into the atmosphere. Everyone knows the story. It all adds up to the realization that the western world is into a deep cultural pathology as we enter the terminal phase of the Cenozoic period.

41

The Issues

From Democracy to Biocracy

But, strangely, we do not want to change the destructive processes of our time. That is where the critical function of religion comes in, where the deepest feelings of what it is to be a human come in, what it is to sustain ourselves in a mutually enhancing relationship with the planet earth so that it is suitable for our children and grandchildren. I have outlined a series of needed adjustments that constitute what I call the emerging Ecozoic era. It is going to require a spiritual discipline that involves a change from our anthropocentrism to a biocentrism and a geocentrism. It will even require a move from democracy to biocracy.

I consider democracy a conspiracy of humans against the natural world. The United States Constitution is a constitution of humans guaranteeing human rights to life, liberty, and the pursuit of happiness at the expense of the continent. We need a North American constitution that would include all the components of the North American continent. All the life forms need to be represented if any of us are going to survive at any acceptable level of fulfillment. The future will depend extensively on the capacity of humans to understand just how we function within the inherent natural processes of the planet on which we live. Whereas, in the Cenozoic, we had absolutely no role in the direction of the life process, in the future we are going to be a condition for almost everything that happens. We cannot make a blade of grass but there is liable not to be a blade of grass unless we accept it, defend it and foster it. We will experience a fantastic shift in responsibility going into this new era. In talking about this transition, I like to use the exodus symbol. It is the central symbol in the *Divine Comedy* by Dante (1265–1321). It is also the central symbol of the North American world. Many people came to North America consciously feeling that they were making an exodus from a disintegrating world into a sacred world. And so, at the present, our most effective symbol is the exodus symbol as we make the transition from the terminal Cenozoic to the emergent Ecozoic.

Centered in the Sacred Community

I spoke recently to some 300 members of various Catholic mission associations. I mentioned that we can no longer have missions simply to humans, whether they be political missions, economic missions, or religious missions. We cannot aim our efforts precisely, and certainly not exclusively, to the human community, because the human is an abstraction if this designation is taken in isolation from its larger context. There is no such thing as "human community" without the earth and the soil and the air and the water and all the living forms. Without these, humans do not exist. There is, therefore, no separate human community. Humans are woven into this larger community. The large community is the sacred community.

The earth is a very special sacred community. Humans become sacred by participating in this larger sacred community (more than the earth becomes sacred by participating in our human community). We must be integrated into the religious dimension of the earth. It is, of course, a mutual process. One is the expression of the other. In my view, the human community and the natural world will go into the future as a single sacred community or we will both perish in the desert. That is the significance, that is the importance, of understanding this larger dimension of sacred community. We have been trying to go into the future as a human community in an exploitative relationship with the natural community without any sense of being integral with this natural world as a sacred community. From now on, that is just not acceptable, purely and simply, because it is a way, not of life, but of death.

When it comes to sacred community, we have in the Christian tradition the idea that the church is the sacred community, and that parishes are sacred communities—as indeed they are. The human itself is a sacred community. Because there is such power in the concept of sacred community, it is being used frequently for distorted purposes. Nations in modern times have assumed the status of the primary sacred communities. We even have the idea that commercial corporations are sacred communities. The industrial world has become the sacred world. We feel that we have an obligation to industrialize all the peoples of the world. If they are left without industrialization, then somehow they will not be fully human! When we are dealing with this idea of sacred community, we need to understand its power for both creative and destructive purposes.

Ecology, Justice, and the Third World

To deal effectively with the natural world, we must also deal with the human world, with the human world as integral to the natural world. As I have indicated, the human and the natural worlds are going into the future as a single sacred community or we will both perish in the desert. It is not easy, therefore, in practical affairs, to establish priorities.

There was, however, a study produced in 1980, when over 700 scientists from over 100 different nations, most of them Third World nations, got together to discuss this issue of human economics and the natural world. They came up with a document called *Strategy for Conservation and Development* in which they said quite plainly that the future of Third World countries lay precisely in their capacity to save their ecosystems. So the ecosystems are the primary context. That is why I say the human in itself is an abstraction, in a sense. The human exists only in the context of ecosystems. We must deal with life in an integral way. In the United States, for example, between 4 and 6 billion tons of topsoil are being lost every single year. If this continues, then there is no possibility of feeding people because there is not going to be enough soil to grow the food. Already it is estimated that by the end of the century, if this loss continues, we would barely be able to support ourselves in the U.S., much less supply other parts of the world. There is no way that humans can survive without fertile soil.

Meanwhile, I think that the "option for the poor," in the way it is functioning at the present time, is one of the greatest obstacles to getting on with the environmental issue. We have statements from the Vatican, stretching from the floor to the ceiling, on the economic issue and on the option for the poor. We do not have anything, however, on the natural world, on saving the environment. Until recently, we did not have a single significant document. The bishops of the Philippines put out a document called *What Is Happening to Our Beautiful Land?* It was written by a missionary in cooperation with tribal peoples. A local bishop presented it to the national meeting of the bishops. They approved it. But what did they do before they approved it? They took out one of the important statements on population. They diminished an important aspect of the document by their unwillingness to deal with population, even though overpopulation is one of the most disastrous realities facing the Philippines and the planet.

While we are trying to be good to people, we are often being cruel. The Philippines, at the beginning of this century, had six million people. That figure has doubled every twenty years, from six to twelve, twelve to twenty-four, twenty-four to fifty. The number is 70 million now, and that is in the process of doubling. There will be over 100 million people shortly after the year 2010. Meanwhile, the mangrove swamps are destroyed, and 80 percent of the coral reefs, which are among the richest ecosystems on the planet, are severely damaged. A third of the soil is severely damaged, two-thirds is partly damaged, and the rain forest that once covered over 90 percent of the area will, it seems, soon be totally gone. Only 10 percent survives now.

So we can list disaster after disaster to the natural environment, all occurring, ostensibly, in order to better care for people's needs. Why do they blast the fisheries? To take care of people. Why do they destroy the mangrove swamps? To take care of people. And where is it all going to end up? In the impoverishment and death of millions of people.

This points to a number of other things. We have to live on the planet, on the planet's terms and not on our terms. Living in the natural world on its terms is hard for us. We want the planet to exist on our terms. At last we are realizing that we had better find out right away what the planet's terms are. We must accept life, the human mode of being, within the conditions of the natural world that brings us into being. We were brought into being by the natural world, and we must survive on its conditions. In our resistance to these conditions, we have evolved a pathology of destruction in our consumer-oriented society.

Therapy for the Exodus Journey

Because of this rejection of the discipline imposed by nature, our religion, morality, civilization, major establishments—everything—have become counter-productive. They are producing the opposite of what they should produce. They are addictive; we are caught up in them and we cannot get out. They are paralyzing; we feel we cannot do anything to improve the situation. We are involved in a profound cultural pathology. Because we refuse to deal with this cultural pathology, we are in a state of denial. What is needed is a deep cultural therapy. It is like addiction. We are not going to get out of this until we undertake the agonies that drug addicts have to undergo in reforming themselves. As with the drug addict, we can crash without recovery. There is death without renewal.

It is within our range of possibilities now to disintegrate many of the major life systems of the planet. God is not going to save the planet if we decide to destroy it. It is time that we got shook up enough to remedy the situation. The main thing, and I find this difficult, is to present the full force of the issue without engendering a deeper paralysis. At times, when I get through presenting the magnitude of the issue, the audience is paralyzed, unable even to ask questions. Yet until people realize that we are in a crash situation, they are not going to do what needs to be done. Only when we recognize that we are in a crash situation will we react to it creatively at the proper level of efficacy. It remains true, however, that we can only deal with people within their limitations of understanding and action.

This question involves some very, very difficult balances. It involves understanding history and culture and understanding just why the poor are suffering as they are and why all our efforts to release them from their situation seem only to make their pain deeper and lead to greater devastation. Much good has been done, of course. But in Brazil, the World Bank, to help the people, financed that road into the jungle by which so much devastation has happened. The jungle and the rain forest are infinitely more productive in their natural state than they are with this slash-and-burn process. In North America, if we look into the past, we find that the Europeans who came here intended to live here. South America, however, was settled by Europeans who arrived to mine metals; they were originally more interested in gold and silver than in settlement. The gold fever has again struck the rain forest region and enormous damage is being done in mining this of gold. Gold evokes a madness in Western peoples who will kill off anything to get to the gold. The natural world is at the mercy of such human frenzy.

Ritual, Religious Education, and Sacrament

We come to religious education. The Ten Commandments are no lonqer adequate. Not a single Commandment, for example, gives us any direction regarding the natural world. There are in the Bible and in some of the ritual books, of course, prescriptions about how to deal with the natural world, but these are comparatively few. Nor does the Apostles' Creed give us any direction: "I believe in God the Father Almighty, Creator of heaven and earth and all things," and then a long declaration on redemption. But it does not linger over creation. And when we are young we learn the catechism. "Who made you?" "God made you." "Who is God?" "God is the creator of heaven and earth and all things." "What are the divine attributes?" etc. In my early days, when I was seven or eight years old, I memorized all those big theological words such as infinity and infallibility. But I learned nothing significant about the natural world. The role of the natural world as a mode of divine presence was not mentioned.

Some years ago, I was in the city of Buffalo, New York, at a meeting of religion teachers. There were several thousand teachers of religion there and wherever you have teachers, you have booksellers selling textbooks. There must have been fifty companies there with displays. I went down the whole series of them. I found books on everything under the sun dealing with religion, belief, social responsibility, spirituality, prayer, ministry, sacraments, the Blessed Virgin, all these things. Nowhere, though, could I find anything dealing with the created world, with the natural world. A person could grow up in that context believing that humans had no basic relationship with the natural world, no responsibilities to the natural world, no sense of identity with the natural world.

Regarding sacraments: baptism gives us a relationship with the divine; it gives us a human religious community. But it is not a fully satisfactory initiation ritual. It does not give us any substantial relation with the natural world. We use the water, but we do not exactly relate to the water. We use it as symbol of purification. We still do not appreciate the water itself. In the blessing of the water during the Easter Vigil, however, there is a rather wonderful invocation regarding the water as it is taken into the world of the sacred. But there is still the problem of leaving out the natural world in its primary role.

One of my suggestions is that we look to the Omaha Indians who have a wonderful ceremony presenting an infant to the four regions of the universe. They present the child to the heavens and to the atmospheric world, to the earthly world, and even to the subsoil world. They proclaim, "Oh ye heavens, sun, moon, and stars, oh ye that dwell in the heavens, I bid you hear me. Into your midst has come a new life. Consent ye, we implore, make its path smooth that it may pass beyond the first hill. Oh ye clouds, winds, rains, all ye powers that move across the atmosphere, I bid you hear us. Into your midst has come a new life. Consent ye, we implore, make its path smooth." And so for the animals, the trees, and the insects; in each case, presenting the child into the universe that the child will live in and then bonding this with the care of the infant.

It is a wonderful word, "bonding." We talk about how parents are bonded with infants when they are born, how our societies are bonded, and so forth. But this bonding with nature is a most primordial mode of intimate presence. If we do not have this bonding in childhood, we are not very likely to get it when we are older, particularly in this alienating, industrial world that considers itself progressive to the extent it isolates itself from the natural world. In fact, in a famous lecture in 1893 on ethics and evolution, Thomas Huxley expressed this very point. "Human civilization" he said, "consists in resistance, and the negation of nature at every step." In other words, the "moral" world is an emergence of the human out of that dark, natural world about us and the taking of ourselves away from these blind forces. To be moral, we must have an existence simply "in ourselves."

Our Fascination with Tragedy

Freeman Dyson wrote a book not long ago. He had a lot to do with nuclear research and is a scientist of some prestige. He wrote a book, *Weapons and Hope* (New York: Harper & Row, 1985). The last chapter is entitled, "Tragedy Is Not Our Business." There is in the Western civilization apparently a fascination with tragedy, and that is why spirituality in the past was a kind of a grim business, generally. We are constantly dealing with evil and good.

Dyson wrote about the sense of tragedy in terms of Robert Scott's journey to the South Pole. Scott (1868–1912) made great preparations. In 1912 he was already using motorized equipment. Roald Amundsen (1872–1928) was making the journey at the same time and both explorers were in a race to see who would get there and back. Scott made the journey with a tremendous amount of equipment. He went the standard way. Amundsen figured there must be another way, and he had an instinct for what is called "sagacity." Sagacity is a bit of cunning matched with wisdom. Sagacity is really applied wisdom. Parents have it with children. How do you deal with a child? You have got to have sagacity, that is, you have to be very insightful.

Anyway, Amundsen thought about the journey and he chose an unusual route. He also chose to go with dogs. Now Scott used ponies, some of the northern breeds. Scott got to the South Pole but on his way back he got caught in a blizzard eleven miles from the base camp. He was caught there for five days. During that time he and his companions died; they froze. He kept a journal, and later the journal was published. It is something to read the journals of this man who recorded such heroism and English stick-to-itiveness, pushing forward, not flinching, stalwart in the face of difficulty, not giving up. This shows up in the journals, the sense that he and his companions were committed to this and it meant so much for them, and for the country they represented, and they were going to be faithful to the nobility of the mission to the end.

Amundsen got there and got back, but Scott became the great hero, the heroic figure. Scott's journals, with their tragic ending, were published in 1912. During the First World War, his journals were read by English soldiers going to France for heroic combat. Scott got all the publicity. Everybody forgot Amundsen. Apsley Cherry-Garrard, a person at the base camp, went out to rescue Scott and found him there. What Cherry-Garrard and the others did was take the journal and some other things and then just cover the place all over with snow and ice, and go back. Cherry-Garrard thought a long while before he wrote anything about it. And when he did write about it, he reflected profoundly on this question of tragedy, and this Western fascination with tragedy and with the heroic.

I repeat this story now, after it was told so well by Freeman Dyson, because there is a feeling that we must press on with this tragic industrial world, that we are committed to it. No matter what it costs, this is the way. But Cherry-Garrard, reflecting on the Scott expedition, analyzed the journey and, in a penetrating final comment, wrote this phrase: "Tragedy is not our business." He reflected on the fascination people had with the tragic death of

Scott; he saw that Scott deserved enormous praise, but, ultimately, "tragedy is not our business." Scott had failed. He did not get back and the role of an explorer is to get there and get back alive. It is a profound thing. Cherry-Garrard appreciated the effort put into the expedition, but ultimately there was a certain amount of failure there. Amundsen went, got back, and nobody paid that much attention. As with Scott, we are caught in the tragic ending of our commercial, industrial venture. But even with death facing us in the collapse of our monumental establishments, we refuse to alter the direction we have chosen.

The New Exodus

Like Scott and Amundsen, we too are on a journey. We are, at the present time, in an exodus moment. We must carry this off. We need the sagacity, as well as immense energy, to find our way into the Ecozoic era. People say we cannot do it, and the answer is that we *must* do it. There are sacrifices to be made. There is the discipline. There is the spirituality. There is a divine meaning in the process. If we do not perceive the sacred nature of our journey, then we will not be able to bring about the salvific transformation needed. We need to appreciate especially the real dimensions of what it is to be a member of the sacred community in this larger sense of the term.

We need to develop a clearer sense of that celebratory world we are entering. I sometimes describe the universe through its vast extension in space and through its total sequence of transformations in time, as a single, vast, multiform celebratory event. What we are aiming for is to be able to celebrate our exodus in a new way. For this exodus is not only salvific in the sense of some eternal beatitude, but also in the sense of moving into a present earthly situation that has its own delight, its own celebratory aspects. In this process lies what I would call our true spirituality.

Trust in God

Many people wonder if all we should do now is trust in God. But

God is not going to take care of our present crisis. The deity is not going to pick up the pieces and remedy the disasters we bring about. God gives us the capacity to deal with these things. One of the most disappointing aspects of Christian spirituality comes from the spiritual classic widely used in the last century, De Caussade's *On Abandonment*, which counsels total abandonment and total trust in the divine. That is all quite acceptable but look what God is permitting us to do. God is letting us kill off the most beautiful things around and evidently God is not bringing an end to it. God is functioning through ourselves. God is telling us what to do. The natural world is telling us what to do. God speaks to us through the natural world.

There is a certain ultimacy in saying that God is our hope. But God does not function that way. The universe does not function that way. The universe functions through the forces that are structured into the universe. How these forces function, and how the human functions, will determine the destiny of the universe. In that total process, there is this ultimate, numinous dimension of the universe that is offering guidance.

Basic Life Communities

I have had a little bit to do with the T'Boli tribes of the Philippines. My connection is with a unique mission there. It is quite impressive the way the mission is working with the people out of their traditions. They have a creation epic, a magnificent thing. It takes twenty-five hours to recite. They are passing from a hunter-gatherer phase to a more settled phase. They have these basic life communities. These are different from those in Brazil, where I believe they have between 50,000 and 100,000 basic Christian communities. In Brazil, people get together and they read Scripture and discuss what it means in relation to their life situation. This has been a part of liberation theology. Liberation theology has its glorious aspect, but I myself would like to see basic "life" communities developed, in the Philippines, communities based on the soil, based on the land, based on the religious meaning of the earth, because these people, as they are educated, as they get higher education, their education is going to be progressively less Christian and they will have to deal with the secularized world. If they established their rootedness in the earth, they would, to some extent at least, get beyond the left-right political division that occurs in most newly developing countries. To get beyond this left-right division, one of the basic things is to deal with the land. This is everybody's common concern.

The idea that we were in these developing countries to help the people there is extremely questionable. Really what the outside help has been doing is helping the rich get richer rather than taking care of the poor. There seems to be a strange mix-up in these matters at the present time. That is why I am unsure of good people; often I would rather deal with people other than the good people. Good people, in this context, are often doing more harm than bad people are. There is a certain amount of conviction on the part of a lot of people (like U.S. commercial establishments) that the well-being of everybody depends on keeping the industrial economy going, keeping the jobs there, keeping the rate of consumption high. It is hard to know if Western commercial people are deliberately doing something wrong, or if they really envisage themselves as doing something good within the context of their mixed-up mentality.

I sometimes think that almost everything at the present time we think is good is probably bad, in economics and in many other fields, such as medicine or chemical-based agricultural programs at state universities. The directors of these programs were convinced that it was good to use chemical agriculture. The "green revolution" in agriculture was supposed to be a good thing, and it proved to be a disastrous thing in most instances. There may be an enormous amount of perfidy to begin with, but there is also a large amount of pathology working itself out.

Christian Tradition and the New Cosmology
The basic role of theology, as traditionally presented, is to explain

revelation as it is given to us in the Bible and carried on in Christian tradition. This revelation carries the limitations of the Bible itself, of the language of that time, of the conditions of that time. It does carry within it a transcultural message but a message that is still profoundly limited by the circumstances in which it is given.

Theology is basically a deductive science. It starts off with revelatory processes that a person believes in an unchanging faith. We do not realize how great the discontinuity is between our present historical moment and what has gone before us. It is always a question of continuity or discontinuity, and what I am saying is that there is a much greater discontinuity than we have ever known before. It is why I say that the type of presentation that Teilhard makes (and basically my position is the theological position taken by Teilhard) is the greatest theological shift since the early Fathers first structured Christian theology. Our Christian theology is a kind of commentary on St. Paul through Augustine, Thomas Aquinas, and some of the other Christian thinkers. There is the tendency to say that revelation is finished at the end of the Bible, that there is not going to be any more revelation in that category. We can accept that. But there are, to my mind, new revelatory possibilities that we are experiencing. The difficulty in understanding our new revelatory experience arises from the need for an extensive change in our thinking. We must expand our capacity to deal with the evidence confronting us. If God is speaking to us through the universe, and if we are now seeing that the universe functions differently from what earlier Christians thought, then we must have a different way of articulating our Christian belief.

We have, in our new understanding of the universe, new ways of understanding the divine manifestation in the natural world. We have a new type of revelation. It is not, however, in the same category as biblical revelation. It must be qualitatively different if it is to deal with the issues before us. Theology, as we have known it, no matter how it is developed, cannot interpret the present. But the flip side is that we cannot interpret the present without it. It is not a question of negating the whole 3000 years of biblical Christian culture, yet, in my view, a major part of the Christian task in that context has been done. Something else is happening, and we are now capable of new and precious insights.

Take the idea of exodus. This adaptation of the exodus symbol represents something more than did previous adaptations. When I speak of the exodus of the planet earth from its terminal Cenozoic to its emergent Ecozoic phase, this is a radically different mode of exodus. A new community, the earth community, the entire planet, is making the exodus. When I express a new sense of what the sacred community is, this involves differences that cannot be simply read into the prior theological formulations. I am arguing for a change in paradigm. Tom Clarke seems to be indicating that all these issues can be dealt with within the existing paradigm.

We agreed that it is a question of continuity-discontinuity of paradigms. I am arguing for a much more radical discontinuity, though history does not permit total discontinuities. We cannot break the chain of life. We cannot interrupt history, we cannot sever the continuity of biological development. We cannot separate the sequence in any phase of the life processes. The life sequence does involve mutations, however, and I am closer to a "mutation presentation" in this discussion. This process will continue, although there will never be a definitive answer to the problem of continuity-discontinuity. Our failure to deal effectively with this issue in our present context, however, is bringing us close to absolute failure in the face of ultimate ecological disaster.

Thomas Clarke

The Context

The Sacred Community: A New Conception
My perspective continues to be that of traditional Christian theol-

ogy and faith, listening to the new cosmology and asking what the new cosmology can do for traditional theology and vice versa. My reflections will be largely centered around the notion of the sacred community.

First, I would like to say that one of Tom Berry's basic conceptions, namely, the universe and the earth as a single community, not only is valid and legitimate from a theological perspective, but also is a key insight, one that we really have to listen to within the Roman Catholic church. It is a new conception. Very often, especially when you hear magisterial pronouncements on a "new" idea the church has fought tooth and nail for a century, the church will say that it has "always believed that." But I would like to accent that this is a new insight. We can talk about a prehistory of this insight, the Pauline teaching of the body of Christ for example. What Teilhard has done and what Tom Berry has done is to extend what St. Paul has written about the involvement of the whole cosmos in the salvation process. Now I say once again, while wincing a bit, that this language, valid and crucial language for us to use and language that we have to use, is nevertheless analogous language. Now I wince a bit because I understand, especially through dealing with my own reactions to what is new, that sometimes you can say things in a defensive way that block off fresh and needed energies.

Perhaps I should not have said this is analogous language. The prophetic voice, and Tom Berry's is a prophetic voice, does not have recourse to fine distinctions. I doubt that Isaiah or Ezekiel talked about "the analogy of being." Jesus did not talk about the analogy of being. So I am saying something but also trying to overcome it. One side of me says that the notion of analogy must be inserted into this, so as to include the earth community and the community of the universe.

In accepting this idea, let me talk just a bit about this membership we share with all the other species, in the earth community. It has equality and inequality built into it. We are equally created by God within a single universe—this is part of our solidarity and our equality. We are equally called to manifest God, so we share the revelatory aspect. We share equally the fact of being a subject and not mere object. All of us in this earth community are endowed with dignity, a dignity which has been given by God and a dignity which is inviolable. In this idea I would accent the newness especially.

I think, for example, of Augustine, using what was a stoic distinction between what we are called to enjoy and what we are called to use (*frui:* enjoy; *uti:* use). Basically, he said we enjoy God and we use things. Ignatius of Loyola (1491-1556) in his famous *Principle and Foundation* perhaps was greatly influenced by this stoic, Augustinian, *frui-uti* distinction between persons and things. I would suggest with Tom Berry and others that we can no longer use that kind of distinction between person and thing. We have to get into the habit of seeing the other citizens of the cosmic community as subjects endowed with dignity. I think the extension of the notion of rights from human rights to the rights of all the earth's citizens is very valid. It seems to me that now every species has a claim and every individual within each of earth's species has a claim on us for respect. We are not to violate these inviolable rights, these claims of all the species of earth on our behavior.

We are also equal in the sense that we have the same destiny, as Tom Berry has brought out. The common good of the universe is the common good of all the earth's citizens. This will be achieved, however, in the "dimension of ultimacy." We have practically no knowledge of how this is going to take place, how what we have traditionally called beatitude or the beatific vision is now to be set within a common good, not just the common good of humanity but of the entire universe. This nevertheless brings us into solidarity with all of the members of this earth community. To sample the aspect of *in*equality, I have mentioned that whole concept of analogy. So we have to realize that when we use terms like "subjectivity," "rights," and so on, we are not affirming them in precisely the same way for all the citizens of this community. I want to say that I endorse this conception of sacred community and agree that there is a kind of a conversion needed for us to extend our understanding of the sacred community to the whole earth and the whole universe.

The Issues

The Human Relationship to the Universe

I would like to address something which Tom Berry has written about—that we now have to listen and learn from the universe, that we have to obey the laws of the universe and to let cosmogenesis exert a certain authority over us. Now here, too, I think Tom Berry speaks with pretty strong language and once again my reaction is "Yes, but nevertheless." I would say yes, we do have to listen to and obey the laws of the universe, but we have to remember a few things about this relationship. We must not forget that the laws of the universe have their peak expression in human conscience. Having now affirmed that humans are within the cosmic process, I think I can say that we are the peak instance of cosmogenesis. I think it is important for us to remember this so that, in speaking about human-earth and human-universe relationships, we do not speak as if humans are outside the process and obeying an authority which is present within an alien process. I think that, in understanding this obedience and this acceptance of the authority which is built into the process, we have to understand that the universe is in us as we are in the universe. It is important for us now, having rejected a certain type of exclusiveness in the human-earth relationship, not to go back to a new form of exclusivity. Tom Berry says somewhere that the universe will look after itself. We are not the shepherds. We are not the ones who are going to cautiously guard this child. Does the universe take care of itself or do we take care of the universe?

Let me bring it down to the earth. Are we called to take care of the earth or somehow does the earth take care of us? We have had in the development of ecological thinking not just a rejection of the notion of domination, but a rejection of the notion of steward-ship. I am not so sure that we can simply dismiss this relationship between the human species and the other species of earth. All types of stewardship, relationship, and caring for the earth are part of our responsibility.

I think once again there can be a false dichotomy in the question, "Does the universe take care of us or do we take care of the universe?" I think from the standpoint of the doctrine of creation, putting it in traditional Christian language, we obey God. There is no other reflective consciousness present in the total process except what is present within the human and what is present in the divine creator. So when we go with the flow of the cosmic process, when we are obedient to what we hear coming to us through the earth, ultimately we are being obedient to God who is mediating the will of God and our human call through all of the earth's processes. I think there is something new in this but there is also something quite traditional. I think Tom Berry indicates, in some of the places where he writes about this, a kind of a continuity with the tradition of natural law. But there are features of this description of human-earth relationships which were totally absent from that tradition of natural law.

The hope that I have, as a Christian and as a Christian theologian, is that I am looking toward the new cosmology, and trying to listen to it. I come with a bias and that bias is the hope that what is challenging to my faith and to my theology can be dealt with, in part, by my letting go of much of what I have considered necessary for that faith, letting go of conceptualizations, letting go of cultural trappings, and so on. I guess I come also with the hope that my faith and theology will be enriched by what the new cosmology is saying. Finally, I come with the hope that what I am saying out of that Christian perspective may be valuable as the new cosmology goes out from Tom Berry into the small communities which will form around his insights, out into the general, concerned world. That is my basic hope.

Let me give just one instance. Listening to what Tom has said with regard to the earth community and our membership in that earth community, I suggest that what has to happen on my part and on the part of committed Christians and theologians is now to extend our notion of community to be more inclusive of the other members of earth. As I brought out, we have to extend our notions of subjectivity, human rights, creational rights, and so on. This has been basically my approach.

Option for the Poor—Option for the Earth

I would like now to introduce something which I have been pondering for several years. I introduce it because I think it is very important. I think in the last twenty or thirty years we have experienced all sorts of polarizations in concerned citizens and concerned Christians, right-to-lifers and pro-choice people, people in peace and justice ministries and people with a spirituality of personal development. But I think one of the incipient polarizations that we really have to deal with is the polarization between people devoted to the ministries of peace and justice and people who have been caught with the ecological spirit. This needs to be a very crucial aspect of ecological dialogue. For some years I have taken that notion which the liberation theologians have brought into the fuller consciousness of the church, namely, the preferential option for the poor, and tried to reflect with it, especially with the help of some insights of Jane Blewett. I would like to throw out here for our reflection a version of it which could suggest that the key ecological option is the option for the poor. Let us see if it floats. Let us see if anyone salutes this flag as I put it up there.

First of all, the option for the poor is God's option. When we listen to the ways of God in the Judaeo-Christian tradition, there is a bias toward the poor. I think what is being suggested today is that this is not just a divine whim and it is not something extrinsic to cosmogenesis; we might say that the option for the poor is a quasi-structural dimension of cosmogenesis. When our vision of what is happening in the universe is informed by this notion of the option for the poor, we can see something that is a recurring motif in sacred history. Augustine says that God chose not that evil should not exist, but that God should draw good out of evil. The massiveness of evil in the whole history of the universe, and particularly in what humans have done to the other species of the earth, needs no elaboration. The gift of God is given to us to use our energies of reflective consciousness to promote the common good of the universe and of the planet, but just reflect on what we have done and on what we are doing with those energies! In the Christian vision of things, however, no matter what evil we may have done, no matter how badly we may have behaved, what is going on in history is the overcoming of this awful waste of our human energies through God's redemptive action in our world. So I would situate God's option for the poor as God's turning things around, God's taking waste and converting it to positive energies; I would try to understand the option for the poor in that context. This is what God is doing with respect to evil.

In liberation theology, that notion of the option for the poor has been developed with the focus on material privation, especially under the influence of Marxist theory. I have tried to suggest elsewhere that the heart of poverty is "cultural disparagement." By this, I mean one human group saying to another human group, "You have no worth." My suggestion has been that the basis of that kind of poverty is not always material privation; it can also be race, sex, or sexual orientation. It can be the status of the laity in the church as it has traditionally existed. So, cultural disparagement as the denial of dignity constitutes the heart of poverty, and therefore God's option for the poor consists in the reaffirmation of the dignity of the poor, the dignity of the disparaged. Beyond that, there is the recognition that there is a special power in the poor to promote the common good. I think that is part of this biblical insight. It is not just that we are called to be compassionate toward the poor. There is also the recognition that, in a very mysterious way, the power for the redemption of humanity has been placed within the poor. Our call is to enlist all of our energies to liberate that power so that the disparaged and the despised of the earth now become the ones who carry God's power for the common good to all peoples.

Now the point here is that this notion, which has been limited to the human species and is now coming into contact with the ecological movement, with the new cosmology, helps us to look at the cultural disparagement which we have been directing toward the other species of the earth. So I think we have to say today that in the Dives and Lazarus story, all of us, as members of the human species, are Dives, and we are now being asked to reflect on whether we want to continue to be Dives or not. While there are many specializations within the ecological movement, it seems to me that primary energy must be invested in the empowerment of *all* the disparaged creatures of earth. At the center of this investment, however, must be the preferential option for the *human* poor, for they are at once the most tragically disparaged and, in God's providence for the planet, the key to the redemption of all the species. As we attempt humbly to acknowledge and relinquish our Dives role, we need to avoid the opposite extremes of either confining our vision to the human poor or of rendering those human poor less than central in our ecological strategies. I am offering that to ask if, in what seems to be a gap between the people called to peace and justice ministries and the people now called to ecological ministry, we cannot find some kind of a common ground.

Ritual, Sacrifice, and Spiritual Discipline
Tipping my hat toward the other two themes, ritual and sacrifice, I would hold out the eschatological banquet. In this tradition of the poor coming into their own, what is held out is the eschatological banquet at which the poor will be fed. What we celebrate when we are engaged in our ritual banquet is the anticipation of that eschatological banquet. The Hebrew prophets had those famous passages where they have Yahweh saying, "Take your sacrifices out of my sight; they stink in my sight, because you are disparaging the poor." So I would hold out the symbol of the

eschatological banquet as something which might perhaps help us to think about ritual. And then that might suggest a discipline where poverty of spirit, the first of the beatitudes, is now foremost in our consciousness, a spirituality that is focused not on material survival, but on dignity. As long as we have life, our call is to honor not only human dignity, but the dignity of this community of earth.

Hope for the Journey

When asked about where my hope lies in this present crisis, I have a brief answer. It may be either glib or trite, but I have to say it. My hope is in God, and that hope can be mediated in different ways. But, ultimately, I think that what the Bible says about not putting your trust in princes or in horses or in chariots, is valid. Adapting that message to our times, I do not put hope in any human movement or any human group. My hope is in God. As far as the future is concerned, I look to the option for the poor. It is that aspect of the Gospel that today energizes me the most. That draws my faith and my trust.

QUESTIONS FOR REFLECTION AND DISCUSSION

1. How do you understand Berry's idea of a new spiritual discipline? What might the elements of this new discipline look like?

2. What does Berry mean when he speaks of the new sacred community? How is this community "sacred"?

3. Clarke claims that there is a genuinely new theological insight in Berry's work. What is it? Why is this considered to be a new conception?

4. Which of the ideas of future hope for the survival of the planet presented by Berry and Clarke corresponds most closely with your own? How do you regard Clark's "trust in God" as a vehicle for hope?

5. What is the source of some polarization between social justice and ecological concerns? Do you agree with Clarke that seeing other species as the culturally denigrated would help bridge the gap?

6. Is your paradigm of the future in theology closer to continuity, as it is for Clarke, or discontinuity, as it is for Berry? Why?

7. Berry considers "democracy a conspiracy of humans against the natural world." What do you think he means by this statement? To what extent do you agree or disagree?

8. "The human community and the natural world will go into the future as a single sacred community or we will both perish in the desert." Do you agree or disagree? Why?

Chapter Three

Christology

THOMAS BERRY BEGINS this chapter with the Incarnation and the insight it offers our understanding of the divine. He relates the Incarnation to the traditional theme of "goodness sharing itself," but mentions the great difficulty of seeing where the natural world fits within this tradition. After treating original sin and relating it to a sense of fallenness in several religious traditions, he shows how the plague in the fourteenth century diminished a sense of the mystery of the cosmos, which had characterized Christianity in the Middle Ages. Later, he contends, in a scientific-mechanistic world, a sense of the numinous quality of the universe drops out entirely. Berry stresses that, as we move to a new understanding of the cosmos, we face not only a moral issue, but an ontological and religious issue as well.

Our thinking, according to Berry, must move into a time-developmental mode, and our christology must develop along the lines Teilhard began. Berry states succinctly, "We have to discover the universe before we will have a universe Christ." We have to listen to the universe, and leave the Bible and the dictionary on the shelf for awhile so that we can truly listen to creation. In so doing, we may be able to devise a new language that will be more adequate to deal with our new revelatory moment. Berry considers that the new story of the cosmos can be understood in Christian terms, if we understand that "cosmic person" is a shared religious concept, differentiated, to be sure, but nonetheless present in the religions of the world.

Moving into the theme of redemption, Berry underlines our constant need for this understanding, especially in light of the pervasive evil that accompanies human history. Although he gives a powerful example of the horrors that existed during Augustine's time, he again stresses that the evil to be overcome now is unprecedented in history.

Thomas Clarke relates some of the difficulties in our christology to an historical preoccupation with the divinity of Christ, and the ambiguities of Christianity's relationship with Hellenistic thought. Theology, according to Clarke, eventually became separated from the living christology of the people. While new christologies are developing today, some of these formulations lose power and energy for Christian life, and tend to drop out of sight. Clarke goes on to mention his disagreement with those who disparage Augustine's notion of grace, and shows the distinction between Paul's sense of evil in the world and Augustine's sense of the world of human evil.

While Clarke highlights some dangers in creational theology and also in redemptional theology, he concludes with a call to combine creational theology with a theology of the cross and resurrection.

THOMAS BERRY

The Context

Christianity and Ecology

We come now more directly to the basic theme of the discussion, theology and ecology. More properly, we are dealing with Christianity and ecology. We are concerned with the basic belief structures of Christianity, particularly the Incarnation—the presence of the divine in Christ's appearance upon earth—and with the redemptive mission of Jesus, a central theme in Christian theological thought.

But before going into the Christian story, the Christ story, the religious story, we need to go back into the human story. We are beginning to revise our sense of the human venture. The human, once considered the glory of creation, is now viewed as a destructive force in creation. The human has become the disaster of the earth. There is even the question now of the viability of the human species. The issue is not whether or not Christianity is viable, or whether any other tradition is viable. The question is the viability of the human, or, more pointedly, the viability of the planet earth in its basic life systems as long as humans are around. This requires a rather extensive revision of our thinking about all human institutions, particularly about all the religious traditions of the human. For ourselves, of course, as Christians, we must reconsider the dominant tradition that the Western world is heir to, our own Christian tradition. So it is necessary to reflect again on the Christ figure.

Western Christianity, even Western civilization, is so intimately related to the Christ reality that they make little sense apart from the Christ reality. The art, the music, the thought, the social forms, the ideals—the moral ideals particularly—are born out of the biblical story, especially the Christ story, the Christ reality. Civilizations generally are the product of some great story; often it is an heroic story, the story of a cultural hero. Christ undoubtedly is the central heroic personality who, at least until recently, was central to the cultural development of Western civilization. Divine appearance in the Christ form is a most striking thing. Yet divine appearance is widely experienced by humans in different societies, in different historical periods, each in a somewhat different form. The Christ appearance takes on its distinctive characteristics because of the context in which Christ's story took place.

First of all, there is the question of belief in a transcendent, personal, divine being, clearly distinct from the universe. Christian belief is monotheistic, that is, it entails a single deity. Christians do not accept a plurality of deities or even a plurality of independent spirits, but, rather, a single deity transcendent to the universe, who is the creator of the universe. This idea gave rise, in the early phases of the religious life of Israel, to the underlying message of the First Commandment: there is one God clearly distinct from the universe and everything else is clearly dependent on this transcendent deity. In this context, the Christ appearance is a kind of contradiction. How could this transcendent deity achieve a real presence in human form? It is simple enough to have divine appearances when there is a pervasive divine presence, when there is no clearly articulated, divinity that transcends the natural world. But when this transcendent deity is the basic point of emphasis, the notion of an incarnated divinity becomes a scandal, so to speak. This was the difficulty the early Christians had in determining the relationship of Jesus to God.

Reflecting on this later in our history, we grappled with the fundamental question of why the divine appears in human form. This discussion was carried out extensively, in the Middle Ages by Thomas Aquinas and later by Duns Scotus (1265–1308). One of the basic positions, advanced by St. Thomas, was that the divine appeared in human form to remedy a primordial evil called original sin. Original sin, in this view, was the ultimate cause of the suffering, the evil, and the distortions that appeared in the human order. Because this primordial offence was directed against God, God had to somehow bring about a remedy for the situation. In remedying the situation, the theological explanation continued, the divine appeared in human form so that the human could participate in a profound way in its own redemption.

There was, however, another explanation presented by Duns Scotus of why Christ appeared. This explanation suggests that the primordial purpose of there being anything at all is divine goodness, and the basic principle of goodness is that it tends to diffuse itself. Goodness by definition is a sharing, a giving of a person's self in an expansive way to others. Originally, though, there were no others and so God created out of superabundant goodness, out of the urgency of the divine being to give of itself. This explanation of the incarnation insists that this self-giving of the divine would not be complete without a personal, divine presence within creation.

However people explain the world, whether they claim it came about by chance or by some inexplicable phenomenon, the world certainly is a fantastic, entrancing place. The mystery that lies behind the void must have an awesome imagination; it must have an amazing capacity to dream in order to come up with such an extraordinary self-manifestation. Call it evolution, call it what you will, but whatever it is, it is an exciting world, an amazing world. When we ask why the world is so beautiful, a very simple explanation is that some absolute power exists that chose to create it out of the urgency of its own reality. This self-sharing suggests not only that the divine could create such a beautiful world and bring humans into the world, but also could become present to this world in a very special, incarnational manner.

In the human order, the divine would have a very special modality and a community would be formed that would, in a certain sense, be an extension of this personality. The organic relation of the Christian community to Christ is expressed in considering the community as the Body of Christ in relationship to Christ, who is its head. Another metaphor is that of a divine kingdom emerging, since kingdoms were at one time the more brilliant examples of social order. But when we think of what is called redemption and the incarnation, we must ask, "Where does the natural world fit into the picture?" It is easy enough to see how humans and the human community could share in this experience and enter into this story, but where the natural world fits into the picture is not entirely clear.

The Issues

St. Paul and Original Sin

One of the remarkable things about the Christ story is that we have four separate biographical narratives. Although they are somewhat dependent on each other, each Gospel is a unique presentation. St. Paul, of course, sums up the whole story in his writings and is thus the primary Christian theologian, the first and the dominant theologian of Christian thought. He is the person who placed such emphasis on original sin. One of the most remarkable things about the Bible is that the infidelity of the first humans, described in the opening chapters of Genesis, is never mentioned anywhere else in the Hebrew Scriptures. Christ never mentions Adam. Nobody else mentions that story—except St. Paul. Why? Because, in order to exalt the Christ redemptive process, St. Paul has to have something that we need to be redeemed from. He therefore goes back to the story of Adam and Eve and the primordial fault. This fault must encompass the whole cosmic order in some manner. In St. Paul, we thus find this cosmological dimension. St. Paul indicates that the whole universe is involved in both a primordial fault and a primordial healing, and this dramatic narrative provides the story line for all of history. Only when we have a primordial fault shared by all humans can we have a remedial grace available for all humans. Adam provides the fault. Christ provides the healing grace.

The idea of the original fault, an original flaw in the human situation, exists with many people. In China, for example, although the primordial fault functions differently, Mencius (372–289 B.C.) tells us that people are born with sound minds but, at an early stage, they throw away their minds. The whole purpose of education is thus to restore the lost mind of the child. So there is, in the Chinese world, this sense of failure, but it is not a sinning failure or a community failure as Christians envisage original sin. There is also this sense of failure in other traditions. In the Hindu world, for example, there is the fall of spirit into matter, into the complexities of the phenomenal world, into the unending cycles of birth and rebirth from which a person is relieved only by attaining *moksha*, or liberation. Through detachment of our inner spirit from matter, we enter into the a-temporal world, that is, the world of the absolute, the world, basically, of the nonphenomenal, which is the world of the sacred.

I would like to go back to the Christian idea of the universe. Although Christians do not emphasize the pervasive sense of the divine in the natural world, they do believe that the universe has its own sacred aspect. For most peoples, the divine is perceived as that pervasive power whereby all things exist and carry on their activities, a power manifest in all natural phenomena. When a person is carrying on a conversation with the trees or with the clouds or with the winds, that person is in contact with an ultimate power principle. This is one of the most basic approaches to the phenomenal world. It is the reason why the phenomenal world is so wonderfully expressed in the poetry of early peoples, and why their explanations are so impressive, as we see, for instance, among the tribal peoples of Australia. Because of this human tendency toward universalizing the divine, St. Paul wants to extend the Christ reality not simply from the personal Christ story to the community story, but to the whole of civilization, even to the story of the universe itself.

The Loss of Our Cosmic Dimension

Before the fourteenth century, Christian thought, for the most part, regarded the natural world as one of the basic areas where humanity came into contact with the divine. But when the plague (Black Death) came in 1347, the most traumatic experience of Western civilization up to that time, there arose the difficulty of trying to explain in religious terms why a third of the whole civilization had perished. In Florence, for example, over half the population died in three months. The people of this period had no idea of germs and no medical or scientific explanation for illness. Their conclusion was that God was angry with the world. They inferred that the world was wicked. The best thing they could do, consequently, was to escape from the world, to be redeemed from the natural world.

It was at this time that the cosmic dimension of Christianity, which we find in St. Paul (and to some extent in the Middle Ages), began to disappear. Redemption, as it pertained to the human soul, became so overwhelming that the natural world was ignored and the cosmic Christ became less prominent in Christian consciousness. Even with theologians, the cosmic Christ became a very marginal concern.

Of course, as we came into a more scientific world, the tendency to see the world in any numinous form progressively declined. The world, in the scientific context, was viewed as mechanistic, particularly after René Descartes (1596–1650) claimed that the universe is mind and extension. What is not mind is machine. The birds, for example, have no inner principle of spontaneity. They are simply mechanical instruments that have been tuned in some way by the creator to do what they do, but they have no subjectivity, they have no inner principle, they have no *anima*, no soul. Until Descartes, the whole living world had a soul, everything had its *anima*. (The word *anima* has been taken by the Jungians and used in a completely different way, but the basic idea of *anima* is soul, and all living things have soul by definition.) Everything lost its soul after Descartes—even humans in scientific circles. Among the believing Christians, however, humans kept their spiritual souls that somehow are being saved by divine grace.

This suggests something of the theological context of Western thinking. This background also reveals how supremely important it is, from a Christian standpoint, to move now to a new sense of the sacred, namely the sacred dimension of an emergent, continually transforming universe. Unfortunately, we are having difficulties understanding the universe as a developmental process. We are at a complete loss as to how Christian thought can contribute to solving the problems we are confronting in any way other than extrinsically. We are seeing the earth's survival as simply another moral problem. In reality, this relationship of humans with the natural world is not simply another moral problem; it is a profound, ontological problem. It is a profoundly *religious* problem. It is the basic issue facing humans, because if we have the threefold relation with the divine, with each other, and with the natural world, none of these are going to function unless all three function.

We are now in the period of the "third mediation." We are accustomed to mediation in terms of divine-human relations and inter-human relations. We have never understood mediation as regards human-nature relations.

Recovering the Primary Story

If we are going to understand Christianity in the context of contemporary thought, we must understand developmental time, whereby the universe comes into being. We must understand developmental times as sacred time, as having a Christ dimension from the beginning. The Christ story, for Christians, is identified with the story of the universe, not simply the story of an individual at a particular historical time. That is why St. John, the last of the Gospel writers, wrote in a different manner than Matthew, Mark, and Luke. These three wrote of the particular person Christ, with only a few, slight indications of this larger interpretation of the Christ reality. But St. John goes back to the beginning: "In the beginning was the Word and the Word was with God and the Word was God. And by him were all things created, and without him nothing that is came into being." Then he says later, "and the Word became flesh and dwelt among us."

It is not simply that Christ comes into the world at a certain period, but he came into a world that was made originally in and through himself as the creative context of all existence. Christ as the principle of intelligibility is called the Word. The Word here is the *logos*, which has to do with intelligibility. The universe comes into existence through the Word. Later, the Word becomes flesh in a particular human individual.

Even St. John, however, was still thinking within a spatial mode of consciousness. St. Paul and St. John both lived in a spatial mode of consciousness. They had no idea of an emergent universe undergoing an irreversible sequence of transformations over some billions of years. For them, the universe was created once and for all, and time was seasonal time, ever-renewing time within an abiding, fixed sequence of tranformations. In the Christian context, there was historical, developmental, human time, but not irreversible, cosmological, developmental time.

The new story, however, the Christ story as we are proposing within this time-developmental context, is very different from what St. Paul and St. John were thinking about. Unless we move into this new sense of time, we will not be present to the world of reality as it exists and functions in our society. That is why Christians are alienated people in relationship to the present world. We cannot accept developmental time as sacred time. We cannot accept the story of an evolutionary universe as our sacred story. We are still looking at the universe the way eighteenth- and nineteenth-century physicists looked at it, as a purely mechanistic process. How could developmental time have this sacred dimension, this mystical dimension, this divine dimension? This is possibly the most significant change in human consciousness since the beginning of human consciousness, the change from perception of the world as *cosmos* to its perception as *cosmogenesis*, from being to becoming. We live in a world of irreversible, emergent process. If Christianity is to survive in any effective manner, it must bring about a reinterpretation of all its teachings within this context.

Teilhard is the primary theologian who has been able to make this transposition, to move effectively from a spatially understood universe to a time-developmental universe and to envisage this developmental universe as an expression of the Christ story. The difference between Teilhard and St. John is that St. John is working in a context where the universe is actively engaged in the dramatic conflict of divine and demonic forces, but is not understood in its natural sequence of developmental transformations.

Acceptance of a time-developmental universe can give to Christian tradition a new richness of meaning. Christian thought has always had a capacity to move from context to context, but never with this mode of discontinuity, or at this order of magnitude. With religious people, the more intense the commitment, the more fundamentalist they tend to be. Right now, what is needed is not *intensity* but *expansiveness*, the capacity to expand the context of our understanding. Once that is done, Christianity can begin to deal effectively with the world.

I sometimes think that we worry too much about Jesus Christ. We have, to my mind, been overly concerned with salvation and the savior personality. This has focused our attention to such an extent that we have abandoned the most urgent projects of our times. We have a great literature on the Scriptures, we have a great literature on Jesus, but we have no literature on the natural world and the Christ-universe equation. The Christ-earth equation has been given little consideration. The focus on a redemptive personality has its place, but it is not the whole story. It is not even the whole of the Christ story. I suggest we might give up the Bible for awhile, put it on the shelf for perhaps twenty years. Then we might have a more adequate approach to it. We need to experience the divine revelation presented to us in the natural world. When a ship is sinking, no matter what the difficulties within the boat, no matter what the difficulties of feeding people, when something happens to the boat it must be taken care of first. Excessive concern with the historical Christ is presently just not that helpful.

I have already suggested that there is a Christ dimension integral to the numinous dimension of the universe. Yet we need to discover the universe before we can have a universe Christ. In this new context, I am suggesting that we have to make a shift in our religious understanding of the universe. We cannot start with the written Scriptures. The Psalms do indeed tell us that the mountains and the birds praise God. But do we have to read the Scriptures to experience that? Why are we not getting our religious insight from our experience of the trees, our experience of the mountains, our experience of the rivers, of the sea and the winds? Why are we not responding religiously to these realities?

At one time, this would have been taken for granted and considered obvious. That is one of the reasons why we do not find much reference to this in Scripture. There was not this present ecological danger. The cosmos, as revelatory of the divine, was taken for granted. This realization has gradually been abandoned.

Here we are with a planet that is being devastated. The manifestations of the divine are being lost and we are still reading the book instead of reading the world about us. We will drown reading the book.

One of the best ways to discover the deep meaning of things is to give them up for awhile. We frequently learn to appreciate each other by being apart from each other for awhile. So I suggest putting the Bible on the shelf for a while to recover the ancient Christian view that there are two Scriptures, the Scripture of the natural world and the Scripture of the Bible. This theme of the two books comes very early in Christianity and runs consistently through Western civilization. Even Francis Bacon (1561–1626), in the early part of the seventeenth century, is still talking about "the two books."

There is also the recovery of language. I am not only going to put the Bible on the shelf for twenty years, I might also put *Webster's Dictionary* on the shelf too. Our language is inadequate. We talk about democracy as the ultimate in governance. If democracy is such a great thing, why is U.S. democracy destroying the planet? Why does democracy not guide us? Why does Christianity not guide us? Why does our language not guide us? Our language is carrying the dark side of the total process of civilization. There is a dark side of everything. There is a dark side of belief in a transcendent deity, which emerges in the question, "How do we keep our sensitivity to the sacred dimension of the natural world?" There is a dark side of the exaltation of the human as spiritual. The dark side is that the natural world tends to lose its spirituality. With everything, we must be aware of the dark side and the bright side.

There is a dark side to our preoccupation with a savior personality. We will get to the bright side only if we distance ourselves for awhile. We must see a larger picture. We need to let go. If Jesus is who he is supposed to be, he will show up. If Christians are faithful to the divine manifestation in the natural world, Jesus will be discovered.

We merely need to move from an excessive concern with the individual Jesus to the cosmic Christ in terms of St. Paul's Letter to the Colossians, the first chapter, and in terms of the prologue of St. John's Gospel. This is the macrophase mode of the Christ reality. Just as the human activates a dimension of the universe from the beginning, there is a Christ dimension of the universe from the beginning. There is, from its origin, a pervasive, numinous, guiding mystery in the universe that is designated by different names in different traditions. The Christian name is the "Jesus reality" or the "Christ reality." This is another aspect of what we can do once we see the universe and its inner, numinous dimension and are able to address the universe in the depth of its reality. There should be no difficulty in the Christian world of seeing this mystery in relationship to the traditional dimension of Christ.

For Christians, the new story has a numinous aspect. It is the only possibility that we have for an integral interpretation of the universe. The new story of the universe is the context in which just about everything functions in our time. We can hardly do anything without this story, whether in economics, medicine, law, religion or any other phase of our existence. We must begin to have a feeling for this account of the universe.

The Cosmic Person

I am not saying that the Christian story is the only story. The story of the universe, in terms of personhood, involves what is known as "cosmic person." Many traditions have the sense that the universe is best understood in terms of a person. The Buddhists have it, the Hindus have it, the Chinese have it; all have this sense that perfection lies in the union, the discovery of the identity between the microphase person and the macrophase person. Even modern physics has this understanding in what is referred to as the "cosmological anthropic principle."

To tell the story of any of us requires telling the story of the universe. If the universe were different, we would be different. The universe must be what it is universally for us to be what we are individually, because everything that has happened in the whole course of the universe is present in each one of us, just like every atom is in contact with and affects every other atom of the universe. Everything has its individual phase and its cosmic phase. This is what enables St. Paul and St. John to speak in terms of the "Christ dimension" of the universe. Now, the Christian speaking of the Christ dimension is different from the Buddhist speaking of the Buddhist dimension because these dimensions are qualitatively different. Still, there is the same basic metaphor, the same basic myth or the same basic modality of thinking when one talks about a cosmic person.

The necessity of Christ being present from the beginning in an absolute way is the premise of this. It is not that the Christ is somehow being "added" to the universe at a later period. Rather, the Christ reality as this numinous reality is there from the beginning. In other words, all things emerge into being within this numinous context. We are not artificially putting a sacred name on this reality. We give a specific name. But this name could be given only after the Gospels came along and we had the name "Christ." Only after the experience of the Incarnation and of the Gospels could we have the name functioning in this way. It is our way of identifying something that has been there from the beginning. That is why St. John could say, "In the beginning was the Word." He says it is there from the beginning. Within the biblical perspective, anything that was created was created in that context.

There are, of course, many forms of incarnation. Humans in many different cultures have believed in divine presence in human form. The Buddha reality, for instance, is considered an absolute reality. There was also the divinity of kings. We have many forms of this. The idea of divine presence in human form is not particularly uncommon, but there are always qualitative differences among its various expressions. In other words, it is like the difference in religions. I do not like the idea that any one religion has the fullness of revelation. Fullness is a quantitative term. It is like saying that a lily has the fullness of what a flower is and we judge all other flowers by the way they relate to a lily. All flowers are qualitatively different. The Christian meaning of incarnation is qualitatively different and fulfills a unique role, but there are other incarnations.

For most peoples, the primary manifestation of the divine is in the cosmological order. The Bible has a sense of the divine-human interaction in the drama of history. So historical realism comes into the Bible. Within this historical realism an effective incarnation of the divine must take place in an historically identifiable individual. Buddha also was an historical person. In Buddhism, there is also someone who is an historical person with a special relationship with the ultimate reality. While Buddhism denies that there is any God or any divinity, it does have the idea that whatever exists does manifest the Buddha nature. But with Christianity, we must have an individual fulfilling that role who must have an eternal divine mode and a human historical mode. The idea of "Mother of God" is found in various traditions. Christians, too, have the idea of Mother of God, but this is a more historical individual than, for instance, in the Egyptian world. In the Christian tradition, it is a qualitatively different thing. There is a qualitative, structural difference in its realization.

Redemption

The question of incarnation naturally leads to the question of redemption. (I consider myself a very conservative Christian, by the way.) We obviously need to be redeemed from the destruction and the devastation that we have always caused. But now we need to be redeemed more than ever. A sense of pervasive evil has gripped the human at different phases. We have it in the Bible, that constant need to be redeemed from failures that are constantly occurring. That is why, in the Bible, there is so much reference to sacrifice and atonement.

One of the things that I will take up later (Chapter 5) is the question of sacrifice, why the incarnational appearance of the divine had to undergo a sacrificial death. It occupies fully a fourth of the Gospels. It takes up a massive amount of the story, those last few days when Christ, who was always marginal to the society, was expressing some extraordinary positions regarding basic moral values, the values of humility and human compassion. He was a heroic personality, not a warring personality; he was proclaiming peace, proclaiming justice, and defending the poor until he was executed by those in power. Now this is all integral to the entire cosmological and human processes. The universe has this built-in disastrous element. If there is any aspect of the universe, or history, or cosmology that is fully evident, it is the role of disaster, disaster leading ultimately to a larger range of creativity. But what is happening in our times is disaster at a new order of magnitude, in a new modality, and with a new level of consequence. It remains to be seen just what creativity might emerge in this situation.

St. Augustine, in dealing with the barbarian assault on Rome in 410 A.D., also had a sense of disaster. People sometimes complain that Augustine was too preoccupied with evil. If we lived in his time, however, we would be preoccupied with evil too, not simply the evil of barbarian assault, but the evil inherent in the breakup of the Roman human sensibilities. Their enjoyments were so terrifying. In the Coliseum, for example, it is difficult to believe the amount of death inflicted on animals and humans. The number of animals killed was so enormous that Louis Mumford, in his *City in History* (New York: Harcourt Brace, 1961), says they are still digging up viscous undecayed matter. The morbid entertainments of that period were terribly degrading.

Christianity at the time was able to achieve so much because it reacted against this horror and offered a sense of the role of the poor. It offered a discipline, a lifestyle, it offered companionship, it offered community; it began to offer a certain number of thinking people and literary writers. It was able to bring about an individual and cultural healing. A new creativity began to emerge. The question of evil was omnipresent in this process and being able to deal with it was important. Christians were able to deal with this because an overwhelming psychic energy flowed into the human process through the Christian story. The new spiritual leaders had the feeling that they were divinely commissioned. They believed they were bringing about a new mode of divine presence in the human community and were therefore able to deal with the tragic condition of the times.

At present, we are living between disastrous failure and precarious success. This is not so new. Only its form and consequences are new. It is all one story, with many phases. But of all the different phases through which the story goes, and of all the different contexts in which the story is told, the context as we now experience the story has an order of magnitude that, in its consequences, far exceeds anything of earlier times. No people at any time were dealing with the survival of the planet's geological structures, major biosystems, or chemical constitution. This might be compared to the survival of Rome in Augustine's time, but to have the whole planet at stake, and to have the power to explode it and literally to demolish it—and to be actually in the process of doing that—is something that no one faced in former centuries.

The Question of Evil
In the natural world, there is certainly entropy, in other words, the whole question of the negative, the destructive, the retarding, the opaque, the dark side of things. This is inherent to both the natural world and the human world. Because this entropy constitutes the human condition, there is a growing tendency in Christian thought to identify the human condition with original sin. Christian thought does not exactly emphasize a single, original moral failure, but rather emphasizes the myth of the fall, simply as a way of indicating that the human life situation is subject to evil and the inescapable pain of existence. In this sense, the entire world has its own tension, its own destructiveness, built into it, but the human experiences this tragic condition in a special moral sense.

Western peoples are so sensitive to this that we might say that in the Western psyche there is this deep, hidden rage against the human condition. We have the capacity to deal creatively with the heat and the cold and the suffering, as well as the diseases and the distortions that enter into life. In the Christian context, "resurrection" (rather than evil) is really the ultimate word. It is the ultimate perspective from which to look at Christianity, the human, or the universe. Resurrection refers to a comprehensive, glorious new transformation. My sense of foreboding has to do with destructive human forces that are cutting short the total process. Humans are distorting the whole process in an irreversible way. Christians say, "Well, so it happened. We are going to experience a resurrection and everything will be healed and everything will be new and glorious, so why worry about it?" But the fact is that we have to worry about it. The new, resurrected world will present forever the distortions we have imposed. We have responsibility for the temporal and eternal processes. That is the paradox in Christianity. We can do temporal damage that is also, in a sense, eternal damage. Understanding this paradox is an ultimate challenge to religious understanding.

THOMAS CLARKE

The Context

Traditional Christology: Strengths and Weaknesses

It is hard to know what to say after that brilliant presentation by the "conservative radical" who is Tom Berry.

These remarks will be directed first to the theme of incarnation, then redemption, then fulfillment or eschatology. I will outline how traditional christology, as it has been revised in our day, comes into the ecological era. Quite obviously, it comes with both strengths and weaknesses. I think perhaps the chief strength of the christological tradition has been its strong anti-Docetist character. Anyone who has studied christology knows that, from the very beginning, there was a threat from Gnostic sources to our understanding of Jesus as the Christ. They became known as the Docetists, those who suggested that Christ really did not experience human birth, that he really was not born of a woman but somehow miraculously came to this earth, that he really was not fully one of us, that someone else died on the cross. One form that this tendency took was that the person who died on the cross really was not a divine being, the Son of God. From the very beginning, as the First Letter of St. John illustrates, Christianity resisted that tendency to etherealize a fully enfleshed Son of God.

The Christian tradition has also always insisted on particularity, on the fact that a particular human being, not some abstract idea or some kind of symbol, is at the heart of our faith, but a particular human being, born in a certain place at a certain period of history. This has given origin to the expression "the scandal of particularity" because there are problems associated with this dimension of our faith.

Apologetically, especially when looking for a certain symmetry and a certain neatness in its understanding of the salvation process, the church has had to deal with the fact that this one Jew, from a particular corner of the world, is identified as the center of human history and the center of cosmic history. At least in the mainstream of Christianity, there has been a strong insistence that the Son of God has come, the Word of God has come in the flesh of a particular person. This has not excluded the idea that the Jesus of history, in the process of the reception of the faith within the Christian community, became the Christ of faith and the cosmic Christ, with all of the power and all of the energy which that type of symbolic statement has poured into the life of the church and the life of humanity. Nevertheless, these grander understandings are always with reference to a particular person, the enfleshment of God in a particular person. It seems to me that this represents, basically, a strength that Christians now bring to this ecological era.

I think that this strength, however, the insistence on enflesh-ment, got somewhat clouded in the course of our christological history from the early controversies with Arianism (which said Christ was not of the same substance as God) and Nestorianism (which claimed Christ was two separate persons, one divine, one human), about the unity of divinity and humanity in the Son of God. Because those controversies were taking place in the Helle-nistic world, with which Christianity was making an ambiguous link, the language of christology in conflict became quite abstract. It became divorced from the enfleshed character of the lived chris-tology of the people in their devotion and faith. In subsequent centuries, in dealing with that abstract and somewhat ethereal-ized understanding in our dogmatic statements about the Christ, the church has found it very difficult to keep in touch with the lived christology of people at the grass-roots level of the church. Later on, especially through an overreaction to Arianism's denial of the full divinity of the Son of God, you had a very strong accent on Jesus as divine. As a result, the worship was directed less to God through Christ than directly to Christ. The trinitarian dimen-sion, to some extent, was also diminished because we were so pre-occupied with an insistence on the divinity of Christ.

All that spilled over into our understanding of Jesus as a hu-man being and you had sometimes absurd expressions on the part of the scholastic theologians. The theologians of Salamanca in the seventeenth century, for example, in talking about the human endowments of Jesus, said that Jesus was the perfect gardener, the perfect sailor, the perfect architect, and so forth, right across the spectrum of the arts and sciences. It was a compulsion to attribute the basic capacity for all the arts and science to Jesus; he had to be the perfect human being. They did not say that he actually exer-cised these powers, only that he had them. Closer to our own time, we had a period of crisis in christology several decades ago as we came to appreciate that the Gospels are not biographies of Jesus, but rather are stories emerging from the early Christian communities.

In their passing on of the story about Jesus, there was that creative element which takes place in the handing on of a story or a myth. For awhile it was very disturbing and difficult for many to come to terms with the fact that we actually know very little about the historical Jesus. There is really not much that we know. But I think what has survived that period of trouble and doubt has been the conviction that the Christ title has an essential reference to an historical person, even though we have no biography of Jesus.

We still struggle with what are the appropriate formulations of our christological faith today. Theologians have not so much contradicted the dogma of one person and two natures, but, as happens very commonly in the life of the church these dogmatic statements cease to have power and energy for our life, and they thus tend to be left behind. They cease to be a language which we speak outside of theological classrooms. I think in the last few decades, that the "one person, two natures" language has just been disappearing from our common speech.

You could take a more recent example. Who speaks of transubstantiation today with regard to the celebration of the Eucharist? Several decades ago, there was a big quarrel about transubstantiation and transignification, and after it was over, the result was that such language was no longer a part of the way in which we reflect on our faith. Something of the same thing has happened with respect to those very ontological statements of christology. We have many different models being offered today—process models, revelational models, models which have to do with the place of Jesus in the history of salvation—and now we will be getting into his place in the history of the cosmos.

The whole question of the uniqueness of Christianity and of Christ has come front and center in our preoccupations, especially on the part of those who have been comparing the different religions of the world, including different versions of incarnation. That might serve as a complement to what Tom Berry has said regarding how we have come to this moment. We have come with strengths, especially that anti-Docetic character of christology which, however flawed, has persevered to our own day. And we have come with weaknesses, as our recently exposed lack of ecological sensitivity has shown.

I have dealt with incarnation and redemption in the traditional way of two distinct but closely related aspects of our christology. I have to confess that when both Matthew Fox and Tom Berry suggested a moratorium on redemption language, I was a little angry, especially with Matthew Fox and some of the ways he spoke about this. I was also rather wary. I guess I still am rather wary of a separation between the creational and the redemptional. Basically, it seems to me, our challenge is integration. Ultimately, I think we have to test our theological language, among professional theologians and pastoral and spiritual leaders, against the criterion: How does it energize people for the task to be done? I think there is a *praxis* criterion of our language. I think relevancy is more than relevancy. I think relevancy is a requirement of authenticity and any language that does not speak to the present situation and does not energize us for doing what we have to do should be left aside. At least we should have some kind of a moratorium on using such language. But my own bias is toward a redemptional language.

Back in 1954, my dissertation at the Gregorian University in Rome was *The Eschatological Transformation of the Material World According to St. Augustine.* (I had never heard the word "ecology" at that time but things come back both to haunt you and to cheer you.) It helped to make something of an Augustinian of me. I know Augustine is not a favorite household name nowadays, but one of the things that attracted me to St. Augustine was his theme of grace. When I subsequently came back to teach the doctrine of grace, I drew heavily upon Augustine, St. Paul, and Luther, all of whom are pretty consistent from the standpoint of an accent on sin and grace.

One of the sources of my anger some years back was when Matthew Fox talked about Augustinian theology as a "sin-centered" theology, which I think is not fair to what Augustine was really trying to say. In contrast to what developed through St. Thomas and the other scholastics, the Augustinian doctrine of grace, picked up from the Pauline doctrine of grace, was a theology of the two Adams and the two Eves. It was closer to salvation history than the later theology of grace. It was a theology which still finds a voice in the Easter Vigil, where the deacon comes out with those extravagant statements and says, "Adam, old boy, what a marvelous sin you committed, it was just great!" It is the celebration of our present creational/redemptional economy as a better place to be than paradise. That affected me very deeply, and of course has given me some biases as I approach the present ecological discussions.

There is a difference between St. Paul and Augustine, however. Augustine was very faithful to Paul in many respects, but in one respect he perhaps was not. Paul shared with his times this understanding of the demonic powers, the principalities which somehow were associated with the material world. Paul speaks of the present world pejoratively, not just because of human sinfulness, but because the whole of creation has been subjected to these dark and overwhelming powers. That is where you struggle with evil. I think his understanding of original sin, at least in the Pauline tradition, which includes Colossians and Ephesians, does have that cosmic dimension.

When you come to Augustine, however, who in other respects (it is suggested today) still has a lot of the Manichean in him, is anti-Manichean in dealing with this question of whether the material world participates in original sin. When he comes to the various passages in which the world is spoken of pejoratively in John or in Paul, Augustine always says that the world is peopled by sinful humans, because he is afraid of a Manichean understanding that matter has been infected with evil through creation by some evil god. Although, in the final fulfillment, he allows for a participation of the material world in human happiness, he indicates that we have to keep our distance from the material world and that we do not share our sinfulness with the material world.

The Issues

Models of Risk

I think in theology you always take a risk, and I think you can distinguish the risks of a creational/developmental model and the risks of a redemptional model. I think a major challenge for those who adopt creation and development as their primary approach is to deal adequately with evil. The tendency, at least of some of the models that I have seen, is to flatten out the enormity of the evil which we experience in human life, especially in our present century. I do not say that it is a challenge which cannot be met or that people embracing the developmental option completely neglect to deal with it. I think Teilhard dealt with it to some extent, as have John Hick (b. 1922) and Carl Jung (1875–1961), for whom evil was a polar reality opposite to good and present even in God. Yet I find all their works lack bite. They give an explanation of evil which says the creation is flawed, but creation is going to get over that flaw, so things will eventually be all right.

The opposite difficulty, for those who opt for a primarily redemptional theory, is that their theory gets divorced from creation, and tends to get restricted to the human dimension, seeking its metaphors in legal and juridical categories, such as the satisfaction theory of Anselm (1033–1109). (Anselm proposed a legalistic model in which human sin, the infinite offense against God, must be repaid by a commensurate sacrifice of Jesus, the Son of God.) I think it is quite clear today that those types of redemptional models do not have the same power to energize as do non-legal, nonjuridical models. But I also think that, in light of the massive evil of the destruction of the planet which we have wrought, we still need, from the Christian standpoint, a theology of the cross, a theology of resurrection.

The Contemporary Importance of the Cross

I often think of Central America and elsewhere, where liberation theology, and the life of Christian communities interacting with liberation theology, have been the major source of the energy which has gone into terribly bloody struggles for justice. I believe that the theology of the cross, the power of the cross of Christ, the power of human suffering and the account of the meaning of human suffering as it has been given in the Christian tradition, has shown itself to contain a tremendous power and energy today. The fact that we have martyrs of our century in Central America and elsewhere in the world, martyrs for whom the motif of suffering with Christ has been their motivation, says something to us. So my anticipation would be that, as we try to stretch our horizons now to include the ecological dimension into our theology, I anticipate that, together with a creational theology, the power of the cross and the resurrection is still going to energize Christians as they try to make their contribution.

The New Story and the Christian Story

Thomas Berry's comments about the Christian story and the new earth story took me by surprise. I thought I was picking up what Tom Berry was saying and thus expected his position to be that the Christian story is just one of many stories, all of them valid, which offer different perspectives on the human story. What is going to happen with the new story from the standpoint of the Christian story?

My own viewpoint entering into this dialogue is that to the extent to which there is a new story, it has been, if not created, at least occasioned or provoked by the new science. My point of view is that the Christian story has to interact with this new story, which I see as a distinct story. I would look for convergence, for ways in which the new story has to correct the Christian story as we have told it. This has happened many, many times before in history. Then we can look at the ways in which the Christian story can both support and correct the new story coming out today, so that eventually it is all for the sake of the human story. So I tend to distinguish the new story and the Christian story, and call for a creative dialogue between the two, expecting some conflict, but also expecting some mutual enrichment, for the benefit of the human story.

Unfortunately, I do not have Tom Berry's talents in the area of comparative religion, as well as in some other areas. I think, however, we need to explore that qualitative difference between the different religions of the world. There could be a danger that the Buddhists are talking about one thing and we are talking about something totally different. How do we talk to one another about the human and about the divine? Can we understand one another when we talk about the human and about the divine? What do I say to a Buddhist? Here I have to reach for my formulation because we have had so many formulations about Jesus. How do I say, for example, that the creator God (which of course gets us into still another subject) has so created this emerging universe that the center of time (and, in a sense, the goal of time) is one, particular human being whom we call Jesus of Nazareth? We call this the scandal of particularity. Whatever communality may exist in the language of incarnation, it would seem that Christians, at least, are wedded to the affirmation that in this one human being, born into a patriarchal society, born with many other limitations, the creator God has freely chosen to center all of human and cosmic history. That is a fumbling for a formulation in which I try to clarify just what we are trying to say about Jesus Christ.

So, what is my relationship to creation theology? Up here in my head, I think I am there. Down in my gut, though, I still have to make the transition, because there is too much of the old in me which has formed me, and for which I am grateful. I have hope that at this stage of my life I will get more fully into the new cosmology. I think now we all believe that part of the human vocation and the Christian vocation is to receive the groaning of the whole earth into ourselves, including that earth which is within the human. Humans are within the earth and the earth is within humans; thus our human groaning and the groaning of the earth are one. And, as St. Paul suggests in Romans (Chapter 8), it is the Spirit groaning through both. That is where the power is.

QUESTIONS FOR REFLECTION AND DISCUSSION

1. How do you understand Berry's phrase, "If Jesus is who he is supposed to be, he will show up"? Do you agree with Berry that the Christian tradition has been too preoccupied with Jesus?

2. Do you believe that we have lost the cosmic dimension of the Christ story? Please explain.

3. What is meant by "the scandal of particularity"?

4. Clarke thinks the new story of creation and the Christian story can independently interact; Berry thinks the new story is the inclusive story. With whom do you agree? Why?

5. What is the difference between the shadow side of creation and moral evil in human beings? Would you agree with Clarke that Teilhard has difficulty dealing with real evil? Do you think this is true of Berry?

6. "The manifestations of the divine are being lost and we are still reading the book instead of reading the world about us. We will drown reading the book." To what extent do you agree or disagree with this claim?

7. Clarke has a striking formulation of a "*praxis* criterion for language." What does he mean by this formulation?

CHAPTER FOUR

The Conditions
for the Ecozoic Age

THOMAS BERRY NOTES that psychic energy, in crisis situations, arises from both terror and attraction. He stresses, therefore, that while we need to feel the terror of our environmental situation, we also need to feel the attraction of a new Ecozoic age. This age will require our cooperation with the rest of the earth, as well as a new understanding of science, technology, ethics, language, education, and religion. We will need new sensitivities in all these areas. He avers that the new Ecozoic age will be "governed by the archetype of woman," in contrast to the patriarchal governance of the terminal Cenozoic era.

After explaining why the industrial world cannot be replicated today, Berry speaks of our need for poetry, the arts, and a sense of joy—as well as a recollection of our early childhood dreams—if we are to have the energy for the immense challenge before us.

In addition, he lists the main "transcendencies" in the Western Christian tradition that implicate it in the current ecological crisis.

Thomas Clarke expresses in vulnerable and profound terms the need for "the grace of shame" in light of massive ecological devastation (by no means a cheap grace), which can lead to forgiveness and reconciliation.

THOMAS BERRY

The Context

The Question of Human Energy

Psychic energy is at the heart of human issues during moments of crisis.

Presently, we are experiencing the crisis of a deep cultural pathology. We need a deep cultural therapy. To assist in our emergence from such a pathology, there is a need of exceptional energy resources. Where does energy come from in such crisis moments? There are, I think, two sources—terror and attraction. With addiction, for instance, we seldom recover until we become somewhat terrified by what is happening. We become so frightened that we are willing to undertake a drastic restructuring of our lives, a reordering of our personal life, our environment, our associations—a kind of rebuilding of life from the ground up.

To do this effectively, there is also need of a dream. Jung frequently expressed the idea that "the dream drives the action." We need a creative dream, a vision. What is causing the difficulty at the present time is a destructive dream. The industrial age is driven by this illusory Wonderworld dream. In reality, though, we awaken, not to Wonderworld, but to "Wasteworld." The conviction communicated in all commercial advertising is that if you only enter more profoundly into consumption patterns, you will attain a certain blessedness. If we will only buy such and such an automobile, a Wonderworld experience is available to us. We need only buy a trinket of some kind or a certain type of soap, and it will take us from perdition to beatitude.

We need to appreciate adequately what is happening in the terminal phase of the Cenozoic. The industrial world is disintegrating. Everything is grimy. In our cities, grime is eating away the very stones of our buildings. The squalid context of human existence is becoming so unbearable that we are beginning to be terrorized. We are beginning to be concerned by the possibilities of the greenhouse effect, which would change the temperature of the northern hemisphere possibly up to 6°, 8°, even 10° Fahrenheit within the next century.

When we think of the order of magnitude of change taking place in human affairs, it is important to think of the physical basis of all things human. What do we smell? What is the fragrance or the stench that is in the air? We are beginning to experience the repulsive aspects of our civilization. We are deeply affected by the noise, by the hardness of life. We do not need to begin with religion or education. We might begin with our revulsion at what is happening. We are not only failing to respond religiously, or to perceive the religious dimension of this disaster, but we are not even seeing what we are looking at. We are not even smelling the odors that are around us. Our senses are becoming deadened. Such diminishment of our sensitivities kills off our religious sensitivities and diminishes our understanding. It dulls our imagination. We begin to experience a deadening of our capacities to respond. I sometimes say, "Don't go to sleep, stay awake, stay awake!" We are like persons suffocating in a close environment. We are breathing carbon monoxide. We have to walk people who are in a drugged state, keep them moving. That is not an exaggerated reference when speaking about where we are and what is happening in the dissolution of the earth's ecosystems.

If I dwell on the physical dimensions of what is happening, I hope you will understand. Discussing possibilities, in terms of religion or ethics, cannot happen unless we are *alive*, unless our basic faculties are intact, unless we can respond with the sense of physical vigor required to undergo the needed adjustment. This is a type of human situation that has never existed before at this order of magnitude or with this type of addiction.

I would like to present, however, not simply the terrible aspect of our situation, but also something of what an alternative might be, the Ecozoic. I would like to discuss how a coherent future might function, what the role of religion and Christianity might be in this new context. I would like to go through individually to indicate the characteristics of the world ahead of us if we would really choose a creative way into the future. Here are some of the conditions of survival in the context of our present discussion.

Conditions of the Ecozoic Age

The first condition is that the universe is a communion of subjects, not a collection of objects. Our plundering, industrial-commercial society is a perfect illustration of what happens when the person-spirit, interior dignity of things no longer receives the reverence it deserves.

The second condition is that the earth exists and can survive only in its integral functioning. We cannot save the earth in fragments, any more than we can preserve any living organism in fragments. The earth is a *single* reality.

We need a mystique of the earth, a sense of the earth as having a voice, as speaking to us. We must have the sense, in our communication with nature, that it is not simply trees or water speaking to us, but it is the earth itself speaking to us. While there is an ancient term for the earth, *Gaia,* that is used today, we really do not have what I would consider an adequate term for the earth.

The human community cannot survive unless everything else survives. At the present time, a new relationship between humans and the earth is being fashioned. The basic reality is that the earth exists and can survive only in its integral functioning.

Yet the earth is not a global sameness. It is a differentiated unity and must be sustained in the unity of its many bioregional modes of expression. We must be true to the earth in the place or community where we live. If we are in the desert, we live in the desert community. If we are in a valley, like the Hudson River area of New York, we live in the valley community. Others live in the Great Lakes community, and so forth. We make our home in these communities, with all the other modes of being, and if these communities do not survive, we do not survive.

The third condition is that the earth is a one-time endowment.

We do not get a second chance. If we kill the earth, it is all over. If we diminish the earth in an irreversible way, it is a loss that cannot be replaced. Neither God nor humans can reconstitute extinguished species. They are gone forever. The Carolina parakeet, for example, will never be seen again. If we kill off the rain forests, they are gone for all conceivable human time. (What would happen in billions of years we certainly do not know.) It took 60 million years to bring the rain forests into their present state of existence. If we extinguish them, they will never be the same. They can come back if the damage is limited, but on the scale in which the rain forests of the world are presently being damaged, they would never recover.

We are working with what is perhaps the most precious reality in the universe—the earth—and we are spoiling it. It is like being born on the moon and coming to the earth in all its grandeur, destroying it, and then choosing to go back to the moon.

The fourth condition is this: the human is derivative, the earth is primary. All the professions must be realigned to reflect the primacy of the earth. Economics, for example, must have as its first priority the economic well-being of the planet. As long as the economy of the planet is integral, humans need not worry. The earth will produce and we will find a sufficiency for our existence. But the most absurd thing for us to believe is that we can have an expanding human economy with a diminishing earth economy. Our human corporations cannot survive if the earth corporation becomes bankrupt.

There is a difference between approaching the biosystems of the earth in terms of human ecology and in terms of nature ecology. Eventually, of course, they must be one. But there are distinctions to be made. My own position is that of the nature ecologists. I include human ecology within nature ecology, rather than the other way around. I understand, of course, that in our functional operations, we are more in control of the human and must produce sufficient human interest in the dynamics of the planet and enough human energy to preserve the ecosystems of the natural world.

If the earth is not taken care of, everything else becomes irrelevant. If anything happens to the earth, religion, education, economics, the medical profession—all would become irrelevant. We can only save ourselves within the earth community. This community (including the human) comes first, otherwise there is no future for any components of the earth community. The more we keep choosing the human over the earth, the more trouble we get ourselves into.

The fifth condition is that the entire pattern of the earth's functioning is altered in the transition from the Cenozoic to the Ecozoic. We had nothing to do with the emergence and formation of the Cenozoic. The earth experienced wave upon wave of life expansion in this era, culminating in the planet as we see it now. We had no part in its early development until recently. But in the Ecozoic, we are going to be involved in almost everything that happens. Not that we can control the functioning of nature, but much will *not* happen unless we accept it, protect it, and foster it. We cannot make a blade of grass, but there is liable not to be a blade of grass if we do not accept it, protect it, and foster it. This represents a vast change in the functioning of the biosystems of the planet and places upon us new responsibilities in relation to the natural world.

We not only need scientists, we need more scientists and technologists than ever—but of the right kind. We need sensitive scientists who, rather than sending us off into some absurd colony in space, have lots of what Barbara McClintock (a biologist, whose biography was written by Evelyn Fox Keller) calls, "a feeling for the organism." We need to have religious sensitivity to the sacred, a deep, emotional, imaginative sensitivity to everything, from the bluebirds to the butterflies, the insects to the trees. Taking care of trees requires sensitivity; a tree responds to things for good or ill. It is not an easy thing to plant trees, bring them to maturity, and maintain their well-being. Whereas trees, at one time, could do all of this independently, they will, for the most part, depend on human understanding in the future. We now have a humanized planet.

Again, it is largely a question of knowing how to stay out of the way of the natural processes and to avoid oppressive, if well-meaning, human intrusion upon these processes.

Until we get this straight, it is most unlikely that anything else we do will go well. Progress, to be valid, must include the entire earth in all of its components. To designate human plundering of the planet as "progress" is an unbearable distortion. Yet that is precisely what we have been doing. What is necessary is for the water and air to be pure, to be more integral with themselves, for everything to "be itself" in an increasingly integral way.

There is also the deeper mystery of the emergent, transformation process. The earth never remains the same, and, consequently, we not only have to take care of things as they are at present, but must also enable them to be what they are called to be in their continuing transformation. There is no "stabilization." We cannot say, "Well, let's stabilize things in an orderly fashion and keep 'em that way." We cannot say this because the inner dynamism of things is constantly leading to something different. We have to have a sensitivity to the role we play. When I say that we must "accept, protect, and foster," I am suggesting that we need new skills, new attention, and a new mode of human presence.

This new role exists for both science and technology in the Ecozoic period. Science must provide a better understanding of the function of the earth and how human activity and earth activity can be mutually enhancing. Human technologies must become coherent with the technologies of the natural world. The natural world has its own technologies.

For instance, the whole hydrological cycle is a fantastic engineering feat. To draw water up out of the seas, to lift it over the continents, to pour it down over the countryside, the valleys, to nourish the trees, then gather into the streams, to nourish the life there and then to flow back to the sea, with nutrients for sea life—it is all a vast engineering, biological, and chemical enterprise. Understanding this is most important. That is why it is absurd that science, as we have known it, builds things like automobile engines with absolutely no concern for how they affect the functioning of the natural world. They figure, we'll build a few automobiles. If a few are good, more are better, until now we have 400 million automobiles on the planet, and by the end of this century, 600 million automobiles, and we devastate the life systems of the planet.

The same with the scientists who so "brilliantly" produced the green revolution, with all the difficulties that it has caused. We do need sensitized scientists, sensitized engineers. Construction engineers at present seem not to have the slightest idea what they are doing building dams. They do not have the slightest idea what they are doing in this larger dimension.

The sixth condition: we need new ethical principles which recognize the absolute evils of biocide, the killing of the life systems themselves, and geocide, the killing of the planet. It is amazing that we should be so sensitive to suicide, homicide, and genocide, and have absolutely no moral principles for dealing with biocide or geocide. Over concerned with the well-being of the human, we feel it is better that everything be destroyed than that humans suffer to any degree.

Two other things are enormously important. First, a new Ecozoic language is needed. Our Cenozoic language is radically inadequate, as we can see from the language of ethics, the language of economics, and the language of medicine. It does not even have words for the type of transformation that I am suggesting. The medical profession is finally becoming aware that, no matter how hard we try, no matter how much technology we invent, we cannot have well people on a sick planet. That should be obvious, but then it is not so obvious to persons under the spell of medical science and its technologies, persons convinced that human health is simply a matter of manipulative technologies. We have been trying to have healthy people on a sick planet and the medical profession has not, as a profession, protested adequately against those forces poisoning the planet.

We must also have a transformed legal profession. The legal profession does not presently have the terminology to deal with these issues of human-earth relations. American jurisprudence is absorbed in inter-human issues; it has little interest in inter-species issues. In relation to the needs of the present, the legal profession is among the most retarded of the profession. We do not have the type of legal structures to begin this new world of the Ecozoic.

As I noted earlier regarding language, we need a new diction-ary with new terms and definitions of older terms. So, too, in edu-cation. What is education? Education is knowing the story of the universe, how it began, how it came to be as it is, and the human role in the story. There is nothing else. We need to know the story, the universe story, in all its resonances, in all its meanings. The universe story is the divine story, the human story, the story of the trees, the story of the rivers, of the stars, the planets, every-thing. It is as simple as a kindergarten tale, yet as complex as all cosmology and all knowledge and all history. There is no reason why the story cannot be told in kindergarten, not in every detail of course, but in the integrity of its organizational process. It gives a new context for education. We need to get beyond the division between the humanities and the sciences. Indeed, these are mutu-ally implied in each other.

One of our major concerns is the development of new religious sensitivities, sensitivities that will recognize the sacred dimension of the universe and will be integral with the Ecozoic era. Our re-ligion now is a terminal Cenozoic religion. It functions within a terminal Cenozoic context, with all the deficiencies of language, ethics and energies of this destructive period. The dominant ener-gies of the Cenozoic period at this terminal phase have been ab-sorbed into this type of religion, as well as our consumer economy, education, medicine, and law. But the change that we envisage is into a period governed by this new Ecozoic context.

The religious dimension must enter into every phase of the conditions I have mentioned. It must be a religion, for example, that will foster a definition of the universe as a community of sub-jects. We are not taught that now. We are taught a lot about the human, but we are not taught religiously that the sacred community is this larger community of the entire planet, even the entire universe. We are not taught adequately the nature of the earth in its real endowment, what it means in its integrity. Above all, we are not taught that there is a certain primacy of the earth community.

Anthropocentrism is a big word and a big issue of our times. Whenever we talk about something, we need to guard against being anthropocentric, or hierarchical. I do not, however, like egalitarianism in the sense of leveling things. We do indeed need equal opportunity to be our different selves, but our roles are different. There has to be an equality of opportunity for things to be what they are, but that does not make an egalitarian society in which members lose their qualitative differences, the distinctive grandeur that each possesses in a unique manner and to a unique degree. Egalitarianism is quite ambivalent in its understanding and its consequences. This was seen in the eighteenth century by the foremost commentator on the American world, Alexis de Tocqueville (1805–1859), the French author of *Democracy in America*.

Regarding egalitarianism and hierarchy, I suggest that, rather than diminish hierarchy, we universalize it. Everything is at the top of the hierarchy in its own way. When it comes to swimming, the fish are at the top. When it comes to flying, the birds are at the top. When it comes to bearing peaches, peach trees are at the top. When it comes to being a person's own specific self, that person is at the top. When it comes to reflective thinking, humans are the best. But just because we humans are the best in one area does not mean that we are the best absolutely. The thing that is best absolutely is the community of the planet, the community of species.

Concerning anthropocentrism, the argument is often made, as mentioned earlier, that dolphins have consciousness. They are far ahead of us in some modes of consciousness, certainly. All the animals are better than humans in some manner. Eagles and hawks have eyesight that puts our eyesight to shame. In certain modes of knowing, the animals are far ahead of us. The human mode of consciousness would be an obstacle, not a help, to their proper mode of consciousness. Yet there are certain types of knowing that are proper to ourselves, through which we are more gifted or more competent. Obviously the attributes that humans have are enormously important. This is evidenced by the amount of damage that we are capable of doing. No other species apparently is capable of the damage that we are capable of, although, if some of the other genera or species disappeared, the entire biosphere would collapse. If certain bacteria disappeared, for example, the world of the living would crash. If photosynthesis stopped working, the animals dependent upon plants would disappear.

The alternative to the Ecozoic is the Technozoic. This is the great danger we now face. If our present effort at cleaning up polution, reducing energy use, limiting consumption, and recycling is all being done to preserve the existing industrial system, it will not work. All this needs to be done, but only enroute to something different. It must not be done to support our existing commercial-industrial order. If we think we can replace the functioning of natural processes by genetic engineering and other such mechanistic control of biological processes, as we are now attempting, then we are mistaken. There are certain things that can at times be done by our scientists and technologists, but we must resist their leading us into a Disney World. We are finally letting the natural systems take their course, as in the health order, where people say, "Leave me free; if I am dying, let me die. Do not give me all that technology." One of the dark aspects of our so-called Christian civilization is that we begin to over-value life in such a way that we end up making ourselves rather miserable, particularly in our older years.

The Issues

The Role of Women
An important aspect of the Ecozoic era is that it will be guided extensively by the archetype of woman. The terminal Cenozoic

shows patriarchal oppression against both the human and the natural. In the new age, the basic symbol will be one of nurturing and being nurtured in a communion of subjects, not one of exploiting and being exploited in a collection of objects. We are speaking here of the feminine in its ontological reference rather than to gender. In the Ecozoic era, people will be educated primarily for roles, not for jobs. We need jobs, yes, but what we need really are people with roles, people with vocations who are following certain instincts for human occupations that are really human, not people working in factories where they do some particular job for money and lose all their human skills in the process.

I was reading something about the aboriginal people of Australia, and it said that every person is an artist, every person is a poet, every person is a craftsperson, every person does everything. Such a remarkable thing. We have professional poets and we have professional musicians. We should all be musicians, we all should be poets. All children should write poetry. It should be our education, the music and dance and so forth. Our glorification of specialization has led to an impossible situation.

Those who have a diversity of functions and are most successful at it are frequently women. They are being narrowed, however, by their participation in patriarchal, corporation establishments.

Four great patriarchal establishments of the Western world have led to the ruinous situation at the present, the four relentless, patriarchal establishments that women have had to endure as well as they were able. First were the ancient empires; second, the ecclesiastical establishment; third, the nation state; and fourth, the modern corporation. These, whatever the grandeur of some of their achievements, have brought us to a ruinous situation.

As women move into the new order of things, they are assuming responsibilities. The role that all of us have is to support particularly those gifts and those graces that are brought by women. The alliance of this with the ecology movement is very clear; the natural world is a world of nurturing, being nurtured, a world of inner spontaneities, of esthetic, emotional qualities that we associate with the feminine. The primacy of objective manipulation has been mainly a patriarchal development. We generally think of woman as capable of a special mode of presence to things. While this quality is often looked upon as soft, as inefficient, it has kept the margin of human life human. If we are marginally human, which is the best we could say about ourselves at present, it is because women have kept that sense of intimate presence of all things to one another.

Coming back to the ecology movement as it exists at the present time, a great proportion of the movement certainly is being performed by women. There are persons such as Charlene Spretnak (author of *The Spiritual Dimension of Green Politics*, Santa Fe: Bear & Co., 1986) and Joanna Macy *(Despair and Personal Power in the Nuclear Age*, Philadelphia: New Society, 1983). I could mention dozens and dozens of names of the women who are into this and bringing a great deal of energy and insight to the movement. (It would be impossible to list these numerous and diverse accomplishments in any comprehensive way.) I would say that in the union of these two forces, ecology and feminism, lies much of the future.

When asked where my hope rests for the future, I might say that it rests extensively on the new vigor, assertion, and acceptance of women, especially their quality of nurturance. It is quite true that nurturance is not the only context in which women function, but I consider the future lies in the nurturing role because it is a primary role for all things in relationship to one another. Nurturance is also a primary, if presently undeveloped, quality of men. My hope that this change will take place springs from the fact that the new context of the human is being participated in so extensively by women. Fortunately, we now have women in the law schools, the medical profession, religious seminaries, all branches of professional training, as well as the ecological movement. Women are activators of so many of the admirable things that are happening. Regarding my hope in the future, I would say the "future" is already happening. This movement is already in position; whether or not we will carry it through is up to us.

The Shadow Side of the Ecozoic Dream

Like everything else, however, the Ecozoic dream has a shadow side. The shadow side of my dream is the upset that it is going to cause. The shadow side of my dream is the suffering imposed as we dissolve the industrial infrastructure in the emerging Ecozoic era. To get to where I am pointing, we have got to go through so very much.

We first must accept life within the limitations presented to us by the natural world. We must lower the human pressure on the planet, accept the human condition, and not think that we can outdo the natural world. We do, in a sense, establish our own natural world. We fashion our niche. We control our environment more than most earthly beings. The difficulty with our use of industrial technology is that we have the cunning to use it to subvert the basic biological law. The basic biological law is that every life form should have opposed life forms or conditions that limit each life form so that no one life form or group of them would overwhelm the others. Technology enables us to get around these limiting conditions. We can overpopulate; we can tear the earth to pieces in a devastating manner; we can overcome the opposition of gravity by building automobiles and riding up a mountain. And so we can get away from the conditions, the opaque element, by mechanical contrivances.

But then, as we do away with resistance and with the opposing opaque element, what do we do? We recreate the conditions in healthclubs and gymnasiums. We go there to burn our energies against the contrived resistances. We work out the resistance that we should have worked out in our basic activities. We now are creating artificial processes for all that.

So the dark side of my view is basically the acceptance of the human condition and making it creative. Take walking. There are few places we can walk any more. Even in villages, we cannot walk. Walking is almost better in the center of Manhattan than in some villages. Villages are often a single, main street with neon on all sides, and cars flashing by. Very few roads remain where you can walk or bicycle. So we have lost the joy of an evening walk. I remember one of the best essays I read by Ralph Waldo Emerson (1803–1882) on taking a walk. We used to be able to accept a certain amount of cold in the winter and heat in the summer. Now we have to have air conditioning and we cannot think of life in the southern parts of the U.S. without air conditioning. People lived there before, but they knew how to build houses that would protect them from the heat. This creativity showed up in their architecture. The secret is working with the inherent limitations of things to make life creative, health giving, and enjoyable.

The Decline of the Industrial World

I mentioned that we need to experience a certain terror at the destruction that we have gotten ourselves into, as well as a certain inspiration and direction through a motivating myth of the future. The archetypal world is a source of guidance and energy. We do things effectively only under the inspiration of our wonderful visions. Another source of inspiration is the realization that our children, our grandchildren, will inherit the world we give them. The tragedy of our times is what we have done to the world which we will hand on to our children. Almost 90 percent of any generation goes into bringing the next generation into being, educating them and guiding them on to the future. Any generation that does not do well by its children is in a destructive pattern for itself and the human community, and ultimately for the destiny of the earth.

No generation that I know of has ever done such damage to its children as my generation has done. My generation, through the major part of the twentieth century, has shaped a world of ruins. Our children will live amid the ruined infrastructures of the industrial world and, indeed, amid the ruins of the natural world itself. We are making everlasting ruins. We are ruining the atmosphere, the forests, the mountains, and the rivers for the indefinite future. We are ruining the biosystems of the planet and handing them on to the next generation, saying, "Well, we had our fun, now you have yours." It is a rather devastating thing to reflect on as my generation awakens to what we have done.

The industrial world that we have made can be constructed only once at this order of magnitude. It cannot be maintained, nor can it ever be done again. There are three reasons for this.

The first is that, when the industrial period was set up, it was energized by the bright, new, glistening promise of the commercial-industrial world. People did not see the dark side, the rusted debris of it all. They were under the entrancement of the comforts made available, the excitement of travel and communication. They did not see the shadow side. It was a deadly entrapment, leading ultimately to disillusionment.

When we consider the industrial world, the managerial profession, education, and economics, we find that they all support the process whereby the greatest possible amount of natural resources is put as quickly as possible through the processing-consumer economy and then thrown onto the waste heap. The faster this process goes, the more the natural world is consumed, the higher the Gross National Product (GNP), the happier we are supposed to be. That is the myth of our times. We do not see, we do not observe, the rising junk, the expanding garbage heaps, the increasing amount of radioactive refuse. We are fixed in a state of denial.

A second reason for the decline of the industrial world is that financially it requires more to maintain it, many times more, 10 to 20 to 100 times more, than it did to erect it in the first place. We do not have such limitless financial resources. We are beginning to recognize that the industrial system is widely bankrupt. The money is not there, no matter how much people juggle figures. The whole industrial system is financially a disaster, and in the early phase of its collapse. With this rising stock market, we are at the crest of the wave that everybody knows is going to break. The earth cannot support such a system. Everybody has forebodings.

We had received a temporary lift from the political changes in Eastern Europe. When the war in the Persian Gulf broke upon the world, however, we all knew that the industrial system was over with, basically, although people want to get the last vestiges of profit out of the situation.

Lastly, the natural resources that fuel this system are diminished. When we put these things together we see the reality of our present life situation. Even the interstate highways built after World War II are now breaking up.

An Energizing Vision of the Future

Besides terror, we also have an empowering source of psychic energy: that is the vision of a glorious future, the hope and expectation and attraction that emerges from the possibilities of life. Take again the analogy of the addict. The addict, in order to recover, has to be sufficiently terrorized by a deadly situation to change, and, at the same time, must be attracted by a dream of what an alternative life can be. We need poetry, we need music, we need dance. I have outlined the basic characteristics or conditions of the Ecozoic Age. These need to be presented as the vision of an attractive world, a world of community, a world of personal attachment. One of the most powerful influences is personal association, the presence of others that inspires and attracts us to be our best selves, to be our true selves. This role of attraction to the authenticity of one's own true self, is immensely important. Otherwise, we are paralyzed.

I deal somewhat with drug addicts and there is one place in New Jersey which is the most successful treatment place I know. Rather than play on the sense of past degradation, they gather in a program where they confront one another in groups of fifteen to twenty, and each person has to go out in the center, face the whole group, and say, "I am a good person, I am a competent person, I am a beautiful person." Then the others go up and look this person in the eye and say, "You are a good person, you are a competent person, you are a beautiful person." The idea is to build up that sense of who they are in the depths of their being and who they can be in the future.

What I suggest is this: there is no model for the individual. Each life is unique. There is no other person quite like each of us. I suggest when we try to think of what to do, that we think of our earliest childhood dreams. Go back to the dreams that you had when you were excited by life, when you spoke about what you would really like to be. Consider those dreams as your basic guide. In this context, the great archetypal motivations come into being when we begin to think of ourselves in a more fulfilling role.

In all this, a sense of joy in the world is primary. We cannot live without joy, and that is why I consider life, the universe, and the planet earth, all as a single, multiform, celebratory event. Throughout the vast extent of space and the total sequence of transformations in time, it is a single, multiform, celebratory event. This capacity for celebration is of absolute importance. That is why holy days are holidays and holidays are holy days, only we do not like to think of them as holy. We like to think of them as extravagant, or decadent in some way. But the two are the same. That is one of the things that religion can give: the gift of delight in existence. Such delight is the source of immense energy. Teilhard himself had one great fear: the diminishment of psychic energy. Toward the end of his life, he wrote essays on the zest for life. He wanted a science of human energetics, and he explored this idea of the energetics of the human process within a cosmological setting.

An Unromantic Theology

I hope I am not a total iconoclast regarding our present world. There is much ambivalence that we are living with. To have an automobile is an ambivalence, to buy a newspaper that destroys the forest is an ambivalence. We are living in a very ambivalent world. My own approach is to accept the whole scientific process, the whole technological process to the extent to that it is compatible with the technologies of nature. There is no going back, but we can learn extensively from those peoples who are still in intimate association with the planet. The native peoples of the world have profound things to say to us. The industrial world could never go back, but we can benefit extensively by trying to understand that part of our heritage, that very early period when the natural world, was not an *it*, but a *thou*. This primordial awareness is deep in the psyche of each of us. It only needs to be evoked.

Henri Frankfort, in his wonderful book, *Before Philosophy: The Intellectual Adventure of Man* (Harmondsworth Middlesex: Penguin, 1966), examines the Near East between 4000 and 2000 B.C. When he describes the difference between peoples then and now, he says that in this earlier period, the external world of nature was not an *it*, it was a *thou*. It was addressed. Human society was seen as an expression of the cosmos and vice versa. This is why there was so much cosmological reference in early civilizational processes.

The Chinese, in particular, set up the whole human process, the music, colors, and court etiquette, as governed by the sequence of seasons in the natural world. During each season, the ruler had to live in a certain part of the residence. He had to wear certain clothes in winter, certain colors, and play certain music so that the human would be in full accord with the natural world. This all had to change with the seasons, so that the human establishment would have this harmonious relationship with the cosmos. If summer music were played in winter, then it would upset the whole cosmos. If the court wore the wrong colors, it would be a cosmic difficulty. We still have remnants of this in our sense of color and our seasonal celebrations. We cannot escape a certain amount of it, but it was much more worked out in Chinese culture and earlier cultures.

The difficulty arose in Western Christian society, which perceived the divine not so much in the cosmological order as in the divine and historical orders, and in political events. The Bible is full of all these historical events that took place in the Near East. So much of the symbolism is political symbolism. The natural symbolism of the Psalms and other parts of the Bible do not suffice to place the human in its proper relation to the natural world. As we seek to reconstitute the human within the ever-renewing processes of the natural world, we are recovering from an alienation. It is a return to integral well-being after a period of decline.

The Person and the Present Task

What is our personal task at this moment? What to do individually is determined by the competencies of a person. We must follow our own competencies. As Joseph Campbell said, "Follow your bliss" (Betty Flowers, ed. *The Power of Myth,* New York: Doubleday, 1988). Properly understood, the deep spontaneities of our being are our best guide. If our genetically constituted spontaneities fail us, we are "rudderless." What are you most happy with? What are you most delighted with? What are your competencies that give you joy and delight and relatedness to others? These questions are what we have to ask ourselves.

Apart from what an individual can do, there is also the question of what needs to be done. In my own critique of the twentieth century, I believe there are three distinctive aspects of this period. The first is the devastation of the planet; second, the incompetencies of the spiritual, moral, and humanistic forces of Western society to deal with it; and, third, the rising, new order of things.

I myself have been working on a change of consciousness, the building of a constituency for the rising new order. There are the activist groups, such as Earth First, that are primarily doing the immediate work and some of the heroic things that need to be done to terminate the present destruction. To aid this termination process, I suggest people vote down any provisions for funds to repair roads or bridges or to build new ones, that is, to repair the infrastructures of the industrial establishment. People ask me what to do and I always say, "Blow the bridges." We must stop

112

the transportation process. One of the best things we could do would be to run every other truck into a ravine. They would hardly be missed. The fact is that in the United States, the infrastructure is already decaying at such a rate that it can never be repaired adequately. Future generations will live amid these ruined infrastructures of the industrial world. It would take trillions of dollars to carry out the repairs that need to be made. Half the tens of thousands of bridges in the United States are outdated, in need of serious repair and replacement, and every year the infrastructure worsens.

The industrial order itself is inherently decaying. Nature renews itself. We can survive only within the ever-renewing processes of nature. We are making ourselves slaves to renewing industrial infrastructures that cannot be sustained. We could maintain the subways or we could maybe maintain some of the highways, but we cannot maintain the whole thing, and, unless the whole thing is kept together, nothing is going to work. Yet we keep on building airfields, for example, although the air is becoming saturated with flight. (We do not have sense enough in the U.S., and apparently not even in the admirable world of Canada, to keep the railroads.)

The Institutions and the Present Task

Recently, I have been concerned with the failure of our educational and religious establishments. I saw in an education edition of *The New York Times* an insert of perhaps fifty pages on summer courses in colleges and universities, scores of colleges and universities, with over 1000 courses. I did not read it exhaustively, but nowhere in scanning its courses did I find anything on the environment or anything dealing with the human presence in the natural world. The great universities of New York have, quite obviously, minimal concern with the natural world. The universities are into the sciences, humanities, communications, and business. Lord save us. Everybody should read *The Arrogance of Humanism* (David Ehrenfeld, New York: Oxford University Press, 1981). Our literary tradition is an arrogant tradition. We are being destroyed by this type of arrogance.

So, what do we do? We all need to function within our own fields of training. The best remedy for the situation might be for everyone to write a poem. Now is the time for poetry on the level of Dante's *Divine Comedy*. Now is the period for drama and for literature on the primordial scale of the great epics of the past. This is a monumental challenge. The early medieval epics, *Beowulf*, *The Song of Roland*, and the epics of Homer and Virgil gave expression to great endeavors of civilization. Yet civilizations were not dealing with anything so dramatic or so stupendous as this awesome devastion of the earth's life systems with which we are now dealing. We need a music that deals with this. While there are some musicians who deal with the romantic tradition of the natural world, we need musicians now who deal with a more dramatic issue.

The Christian Context of the Ecological Crisis

The whole of Western civilization is profoundly affected by the biblical Christian tradition. Christianity is profoundly involved, not as a direct cause, but as setting up the context. (Even Western secularization is a Christian-derived phenomenon.)

We might begin with belief in God. Our difficulties seem to begin there. The divine, once perceived as a pervasive divine presence throughout the phenomenal world, was constellated in the Bible in a transcendent, monotheistic deity, a creator of the world with a covenant relationship with a special people. Covenant is a legalistic metaphor, an agreement. But what is more important is that we appear to give up that primordial, inherent relationship between the human and the divine within the natural order of things. To give up that immediacy in favor of a transcendent deity related by covenant has done something profound to our relationship with the natural world, even when the natural world is explained as good and as created by the divine. The Genesis creation narrative states that each part of creation is good. At the end of the narrative, it is declared "very good." But this is different from having a sacred, natural world with an all-pervasive divine presence. That is the context of desacralization that we have.

A second Christian element is the exaltation of the human as a spiritual being to the exclusion of the spiritual dimension of earthly beings. In Western Christian thought, the human is so special that the human soul has to be created directly by the divine in every single case. In a sense, that is an honor—to be directly created by the divine, to have a human soul that cannot emerge within the processes of the natural world. Essentially there is a feeling that the human is so special that it does not really belong to the inherent processes of the natural world. This contributes to our sense of alienation from the natural world.

The third thing is redemption out of the world; our destiny is not identical with the world. Redemption is thought of as some kind of out-of-this-world liberation. Not only Christianity, but many other religions, such as Hinduism, have this same stance of release from the natural world. Adding to this is Descartes, a very devout Christian, who developed the idea that the non-human world is a mechanism. So we get an external, mechanistic world.

We have, then, four of what I call "transcendencies"— transcendent deity, transcendent human, transcendent redemption, transcendent mind. We also have transcendent technology, which enables us to evade the basic biological laws of the natural world. And we have not only a transcendent technology, but also a transcendent destiny or transcendent goal, a millennial vision in which, within history, we get beyond the human condition. This millennial vision, or "beatitude," will be achieved in history. Such a transcendent goal arose out of the millennial vision at the end of the Book of Revelation, which promised there would come a time when the dragon would be chained for a thousand years (a millennium), and there would be peace, justice, and abundance under the reign of the saints. After that period of 1000 years, the vision augurs, the earthly Jerusalem will be taken off into eternal beatitude.

This vision, this great driving force within Western civilization, has made us radically unhappy with our human condition, so radically unhappy that it evokes, in the Western psyche, a deep, hidden rage against the human condition. We are especially sensitive to our situation because we have learned that there is a possibility and a divine guarantee of a situation in which we would transcend our human condition.

Other peoples deal with the human condition mainly by strengthening their inner capacity to deal with it. That is why we often marvel at other people, particularly impoverished peoples. Why are they so happy amid such difficulties of life? They have developed a way of dealing with life creatively from within the structure of their own inner development. What do we do? We decide that we cannot accept the disciplines that strengthen from within. We want to control the outside, we want to change things. We want to control the very structure and functioning of the natural world. We want air conditioning in summer. We want heating in winter. We do not want to experience heat, we do not want to experience cold. In travel, we do not want the difficulty of walking, we want to float along on artificial power. We do not want to walk up stairs, we want to be lifted by mechanical power. It looks so attractive, but once we start on that, we begin to build this whole artificial world, and pretty soon we cannot do without it.

Modern industry does not arise simply out of a scientific or a technological basis. The dynamism comes from the vision that comes out of the tradition itself. In trying to deal with the power of a millennial vision, which is really where the problem is, we think that we can force the natural world to function according to our desires. Eventually we must discover how to live in accord with the natural world. So, in these transcendencies, we have the context in which Western alienation takes place between the human and the natural world.

Also, in the East and West, there is a difference in relating the part and the whole. In the Western context particularly, we have developed the idea that parts make wholes. A person reads in Thomas Hobbes (1588-1679) that humans are in conflict with each other and the state is needed to reconcile humans and we get what is called the Leviathan, the state as artificial person. The state as the new Leviathan controls everybody. This contract of individuals makes society. Society is a contract. Persons belong to the society as members of a contract. In the West, the parts are the reality and the whole is adventitious. In the East, the parts come into being within the whole. They are articulated within the whole, and the whole is prior to the part. The part is derivative, the whole is primary. In the West, on the other hand, the part is primary, the whole derivative. Again, that sets up a context in which the human has an alienated relationship with the natural world. This individualism, this privatization, is possible in the West in a way in which it is not possible in most other societies.

Individualism is a word invented by Alexis de Tocqueville in the 1830s. He observed a tendency toward this special emphasis on the individual and on individual rights in the United States. Much can be said for this emphasis. It has a good side and a bad side. The emphasis on the individual has wonderful benefits: its freedoms are magnificent. But individualism tends to destroy the feeling of organic unity and public responsibility. On the other hand, where the individual comes into being within the society, the way a fetus develops its different members (which is the best analogy for the more traditional societies of the East), the individual comes into being having a functional unity within the community. This leads to the question of private property.

During a visit to Costa Rica, I went into the tropical rain forest with a government official. In certain areas I observed that timber was being cut. I asked, "How can you let timber be cut on the watershed here which is so vital to the whole region?" He said, "Private property. We cannot interfere with private property." I said, "That seems to be extreme." (I never expected to find that in Costa Rica.) Costa Rica in some ways is very well developed, but it has not really protected its forest as much as some people think. Its forests are extensively devastated. We passed another group of people on the road who were carrying boxes. I asked what was in those boxes. They were birds. I asked him, "Should that be permitted?" And he said, "They capture them on private property, and we cannot interfere with it. It's in our constitution." A person can wonder, though. The areas of the world that are under private property have devastated the planet considerably, but then we have on the other hand the socialist world that has often done worse, as we see in Eastern Europe.

Behind all this is the Christian, humanist-derived, Western world with its historical realism. The Bible introduces the historical realism that has given this dynamism toward developmental processes. It belongs to the special genius of the West to change things, to commit itself to action on this intensive scale. When the West does something, it does it in a very powerful way. Once the West decides to go into munitions and warfare, look at all we do. If we decide to explore the world, if we decide to put up industry, we do it with a vengeance, as it were. We have this type of energy, this type of genius, and it comes ultimately from our religious traditions—that is why the West is dangerous.

The West, it seems, is the most dangerous force on the planet. The Bible may be among the most sublime books in the world, but it may also be the most dangerous. It has great possibilities for good, and has done a stupendous amount of good. It has brought enormous achievements in the course of the centuries. Yet we must now re-evaluate these achievements to see what has been a blessing and what has not been a blessing. At one time we thought that the blessings that we brought, the religious insights that we imposed on people, justified all the afflictions that we imposed on them. We are now re-evaluating our Western Christian presence in the world. We are finally beginning to appreciate the deadly aspect of our civilization, the dangerous aspects of our religious tradition. These need to be clearly identified. There is also a positive, Western creativity, if we can manage it properly. But that is still to be demonstrated.

Going back to the motivations that give us the requisite energy to effect the new age, an interviewer from some publication asked me personally, "Why do you do all this?" My reply was simply, "The children." I cannot bear to leave to the children a planet any more desolated than I can help. So I say simply that I do it "for the children."

Thomas Clarke

The Context

Traditional Anxieties

I would like to recall Tom Berry's point that anxiety about our own future led us to deal with animistic religions in a certain way.

I can testify what anxiety does in the present moment in dealing with animism, feminism, and also a third movement in the field of world religions which is raising questions about the uniqueness of Christianity. I happen to be one of those persons that Teilhard described as a "waverer," someone who wants to remain open to what is new, open to the truth which lies ahead of us, but yet feels that the treasure of the past may be endangered by what is new. I have experienced a great deal of anxiety with respect to all three of these movements.

I think a key theological affirmation that helps us to deal with the crisis in the church with respect to all three of these movements is the distinction between faith and culture. I think the ordination of women is a major instance of something experienced as a threat. But I think that as we get into genuine dialogue, we will be able to sort out what is the identity of the Christian faith and what is a cultural trapping. Now that is easier said than done, and my sense is that it is only after the crisis has been resolved that there is clarity with respect to what the resolution is to be. I think that, as we go into these questions, there is no way of knowing in advance what language, forms, and structures are going to emerge. Whether we are anxious or not, whether we are enthusiastic or not, about these new developments, I would think that all of us have to keep a certain openness, since we do not know what is going to emerge out of this type of struggle. By that I do not mean that we enter into dialogue without convictions. In fact, I think it is the coexistence of deep conviction and deep commitment with an openness to having our minds changed, that very, very difficult integration of two very opposite things, that is being asked of us with respect to all three of those areas today.

The Issues

The Grace of Shame

One of the questions that Tom Berry and I felt we should get into is very difficult for a Christian theologian to accept as a question: why has this devastation of the planet happened in a Christian civilization, and within a Christian view of life? It seems to me that if there is to be the kind of conversion, *metanoia*, that Tom is proclaiming here, we have to live with this question, and not be too glib in trying to deal with it. I hope that I myself will not be glib. Where these remarks will lead is something that has been in my mind for quite awhile—"the grace of shame." Along with the energies of dreaming hope and the energies of terror that Tom Berry has highlighted, I think the grace of shame is very important. I personally feel that we humans, we Westerners, we North Americans, we Christians have to ask for the grace to be ashamed of ourselves. I will try to orchestrate that in just a moment.

I cannot deal with this question of the relationship between Christianity and planetary devastation in terms of comparative religion. I cannot compare what Christians have done to the planet to what other groups have or have not done. Tom Berry is the one who would have to comment on that. But I have been reflecting on this, and it seems to me that, once again, proceeding from my faith, I do accept the scandal that the earth has suffered more from Christians than from any other religious group. Now I myself am not capable of making that kind of analysis, but if those like Tom Berry who are competent, come to that kind of conclusion, not only can I live with that conclusion, but I think that it could be a case of God writing straight with crooked lines. It can be a call on my part and our part to conversion.

I think we have to let this area of our shameful conduct, this scandal of what we have done to the earth, coalesce with other areas around this "winter of our life in the church," as Karl Rahner has called it in a posthumously published work. There are other shames, the shame of our treatment of the Jews, the anti-Semitism down the centuries, the shame of the treatment of women in the church, and the shame coming from what happened during the colonization process, which I think interacts with this whole ecological question.

Does Christianity now stand under judgment as to whether the power it has exercised on this earth has been a beneficent power or a malevolent power? Has Christianity been a blessing or a curse to this earth? That is a very, very hard question for me, but I am grateful that at least I have come to the point where I can really listen to it in God's presence as a question.

Here are some of the things I would like to say just briefly in dealing with that question, and I hope I will not be glib. I think we must accept God's judgment and the judgment of the earth. I think that grace is what is being offered to us here. Our God is a merciful God, but mercy and truth embrace, and if we want the mercy, we must also stand under the judgment and must accept it.

As we grapple with this question, I think we need to recognize that responsibility is linked to awareness. I am not interested in guilt-trips for myself or for anyone else. I think no generation is to be judged on what it was more or less innocently unaware of. There is a sense in which, in past centuries, we were unaware. Even in our present time, we are unaware. There is consolation in that prayer of Jesus on the cross: "Father, forgive them, for they do not know what they are doing." Karl Rahner has a little essay, a very beautiful little meditation, on those words of Jesus, and Rahner says, "Yes, we knew, we really did know." But I think in trying to deal with the question, we certainly cannot be judgmental about our ancestors. We cannot attribute to them the kind of awareness which has come into our life at the present time.

I think we have to acknowledge, too, that the most intense devastation of the earth took place in a period when through secularization, a split between public and private increasingly took place, and the Christian church, in large part, had been relegated to the private dimensions of life. In North America, this still obtains to a great extent today. These battles we have had about church and state have their matrix in the whole secularization process of recent centuries. It does not absolve us of guilt, but I think it is a factor to be considered. The church has not had the kind of power in society which it had, for instance, in the feudal period.

Next, I think we have to say that Christianity should be judged most of all by those who have accepted it. If we want to look at Christian responsibility for the world, we have to look at those who really lived the Christian life. G.K. Chesterton (1874–1936) had that statement, "Christianity has not failed, it has not been tried." That can be a glib statement, but I think we really do have to look to the saints. Of course, there is ambivalence in the saints, because personally they lived the Gospel, but, to a great extent, most of the saints assimilated the cultural sin of their times. When we get outside the area of personal holiness and personal generosity and look at the more objective side of the behavior of the saints, then it is a very ambiguous picture. Nevertheless, I think we have to look especially to the saints in trying to get a picture of what a blessing Christianity has been, as well as what harm Christianity has done.

As a theologian, with the realization of what we Christians have done to contribute to the disaster and to the crisis, I think I can say that our present predicament has to now send us back to the promise of Christ: "I will be with you all days till the end of the world." (Matthew 28:20) I think our present crisis now gives us a vantage point to look for further understanding of what that means. We really do not fully know what the promise of Christ is. We will never finish our understanding of what Christ has said because we will never finish living in history, and each new situation in history is giving us a perspective from which we can look back, within that whole hermeneutical process, to try to understand the meaning of the Gospel.

I am saying that this is a particular crisis situation that now is giving us a vantage point from which we can begin to understand the Gospel. As Ignatius of Antioch, that early martyr, said so beautifully on his way to death, "Now I am beginning to be a disciple." I think that is true of us always, that we are just beginning to understand what it means to be a disciple of Christ. We have to be open to revision of our understanding of what it means to be a Christian.

Those are some of the considerations which I think enter into the kind of examination of conscience or consciousness with respect to whether Christianity has been blessing or curse. Now I have been talking just about the curse, I have not gone into the way in which Christianity has been a blessing, and it certainly has been a blessing, especially the lives of the saints.

I think this all leads up to our need for acknowledgment, our need to confess to one another, to God and to the earth, that we have sinned, and to look for forgiveness and reconciliation. That leads me to this theme of what I would call ecological shame, which may sound a bit bizarre, and perhaps it is a bit bizarre. But because I have functioned largely as a spiritual theologian trying to reflect on how the Gospel has consequences in living a spiritual life, this theme of shame has really come to me recently as something which we have to let emerge in our present life. I think most of us have been brought up by our knowledge of modern psychology to look upon shame as a no-no, because in the literature, shame most often occurs as neurotic shame, something which has been induced in the family process and which is crippling and haunting people. But I would suggest that, as with all the emotions, this emotion certainly has a neurotic form, but it can also take a healthy form. There can be a grace of shame.

Those of you familiar with the *Spiritual Exercises* of Ignatius of Loyola know that shame is the very first grace that he has people ask for. Until this year, I had never appreciated that and found it impossible to pray for that grace. Ignatius asks you to contemplate sin and to pray for the grace of shame and confusion, which is what he experienced himself in his conversion process. I am talking here about shame as a grace, and of course it is a very delicate thing. There is a whole psychological dynamic. Not everyone is at the stage of life when it is safe to ask for this grace. Someone who has been struggling with neurotic shame may have to wait awhile before the moment has come to ask for this kind of shame. But I think that what we are being called to individually and ecclesiatically is to find ways of sharing our sense of shame for afflicting ourselves and others.

I have been thinking especially in terms of clerics in the Roman Catholic church recently because I belong to that particular body. One of the burdens of being a priest, a cleric, in the church today is that we priests are part of a church, which, through its behavior in different dimensions of its life, is challenging us in our membership in the church and in the ways in which we represent the church. Especially in the past decade or so, after the bright promise of Vatican II, we, in our representative role, have had to deal with the church's relationship with women, and with the whole question of free speech in the church. As a Jesuit, I have had to deal with the dismissal of Fathers Fernando Cardenal, John McNeill, Bill Callahan, and others. I do not feel much like a victim and someone anguished who needs a lot of sympathy, but I think that we priests, and people in a representative role in the church, have to find ways in which there is a place to acknowledge a particular expression of our grief and shame because of our association with the church.

Shame which does not lead to acting with integrity, with authenticity, is a false shame, so the grace I am talking about here is really no small grace. It is needed especially in order to represent the church, but I think all of us share the need of this kind of grace. I think we have to find ways in which we can share, if we feel it, this sense of being involved in something which is shameful. I think that we need new forms of the penitential rite. I think the necessity of rituals is important here.

Reading the Scriptures out of this present experience, I have been amazed recently at the frequency of that theme of shame and glory in the Psalms, in the prophets, Jeremiah and so on, and in the life of Jesus. This ties in very much with that notion of the option for the poor, the culturally disparaged, the people who have been put to shame. I am thinking, for example, of the very powerful Lamentations of Jeremiah, which we used during Holy Week Tenebrae services, in which Jerusalem, that woman, is sitting desolate with no one to mourn for her. She is without her children, a very shameful condition. What would it be like to read passages like that from the viewpoint of a shame that we have inflicted on our mother earth? That would be just an example. How do we go back to the cross of Christ, which has been so powerful in our Christian history, and see how that cross comes into this situation of shame? We could see how it speaks to us.

Some verse just popped into my head earlier today that an Irish poet, Oliver Mary Plunkett, wrote:

I see his blood upon the rose, and in the stars, the glory of his eyes;
His body gleams amid eternal snows; his tears fall from the skies.

I find that somewhat sentimental, perhaps, but it is still a kind of ecological version of Christ. Or, take that lament of the Tenebrae service: "My people, what have I done to you that you have treated me this way?" If we let that come from the crucified Christ, Christ as he-she has been crucified in the earth, it seems to me that the grace of shame that we need to feel would be facilitated.

Finally, I think of those magnificent chapters, Chapters 11–13 in Hebrews. The whole letter is for Christians who have become disturbed and doubtful and have lost energy. They are wondering whether this new way of life really has power. The author of the Letter to the Hebrews holds out to them the example of the heroes and heroines of the biblical covenant, Abraham, Sarah, and the rest. The author writes, "This is the example that you are to follow" and holds up Christ crucified. Then, in Chapter 13, the author writes, "Therefore let us go forth to him, outside the camp." The reference here is to the scapegoat, the one on whom the sins of the people were dumped; in this atonement process, the people were healed and reconciled. "Go forth to him outside the camp and bear the abuse he endured, for here we have no lasting city, but seek the city which is to come."

Now, in seeking the city that is to come (Tom Berry especially has been sensitive to this), there has been a kind of eschatological hope which entails disengagement from the earth, disengagement from the human process, in short, an escapist eschatology, but I do not think that is what the author is calling for here. The author is calling, rather, for a passionate engagement. I think that is what is at the heart of Teilhard's and Tom Berry's call—passionate engagement—and we are trying to orchestrate the kind of resources that we have for this passionate engagement in this motif of shame and glory, identified with Christ Jesus crucified on a cross and risen unto glory.

Of course, there is always a back and forth between present realization and the future. That's why I think "maranatha" is so powerful in the life of the church. John Henry Newman (1801-1890) has a beautiful statement about that being a sign of the authenticity of Christianity. But that yearning for the "not yet," as Tom Berry has indicated, can be treacherous because it can lead us to disengagement. This is what Teilhard was all about. We need to go *through* earthly reality.

The Roman Catholic Church

Regarding the church dealing with this process of modernization and secularization, I have found helpful what Joe Holland has done in picking up from Gibson Winter the notion of different root metaphors (James Hug, ed., *Tracing the Spirit*, New York: Paulist, 1983). Joe talks about three stages of the Roman Catholic church's response to modernity, or to industrialization. The first was a feudal response. The church, wedded to a feudal society organized around the organic metaphor, resisted the industrial revolution and, more generally, the process of modernization. Secondly, the church gingerly began to come to terms with modernization because it was being overwhelmed by it. It decided, "If you can't beat 'em, join 'em." Thus the church, in the second period, entered into the second metaphor which Holland describes as mechanistic. Thirdly, in suggesting the postmodern movement, he suggests an artistic metaphor. I found this very helpful for describing the reaction of the church to modernity.

I think we are experiencing in the Roman Catholic church today all three of these ways of dealing with modernity. In our central leadership in Rome, there is still a good deal of the feudal outlook. I think if you looked at the church's social teaching in the present century, it has been very critical of capitalism, which emerged in the period of the mechanistic metaphor. But it was critical of it from a premodern, not a postmodern, standpoint. I think you can view some of the documents of the U.S. bishops, such as the peace pastoral and the economics pastoral, as a coming to terms with the mechanistic root metaphor, with the modern liberal secularized society, and accepting the reality of separation of church and state, but now insisting on being a partner in the dialogue. Where the movement into a postmodern point of view is taking place is more at the grassroots, in the emergence of basic communities and so on.

In the third phase, the church once again becomes a public actor and I think the U.S. bishops and the leadership of other churches now have been challenging that privatization of the role of the churches in modern society, and are insisting, not on going back to a union of church and state, but rather that, in American society, the churches have a part in the public dialogue. So I have found that model helpful.

QUESTIONS FOR REFLECTION AND DISCUSSION

1. Do you think, as Berry suggests, that the terror of the present and the attraction of the future are the motivations for people to solve this present ecological crisis? Why or why not? What new ethical principles will we need to confront this crisis?

2. Berry has suggested putting both the Bible and the dictionary on the shelf for awhile. What do you think of that proposal? Can you give examples of what new language we need to move into the Ecozoic Age?

3. In what sense does Berry approve of "hierarchy"? Why do you think he adopts such an approach?

4. What do you think is meant by Berry's claim that the Ecozoic era will be governed by the "archetype of woman." To what extent do you agree with Berry's assessment of the importance of women's gifts for the future of the planet?

5. Is the present task of reshaping our world as large, in your view, as Berry thinks it is? Are there any other areas that need to be transformed that Berry has not included? If so, what are they?

6. What links between transcendence in the Christian tradition and the ecological crisis does Berry emphasize?

7. Of our present crisis, Berry writes: "It is something like being in a lifeboat. There may be problems of distribution of food, there may be people that need medical care, but if something happens to the boat, the boat has to be taken care of immediately or else everything else becomes irrelevant. If the earth is not taken care of, everything else becomes irrelevant." What is your response to this analogy?

8. Tom Clarke speaks of "our need for acknowledgment, our need to confess to one another, to God and to the earth, that we have sinned, and to look for forgiveness and reconciliation." How would you respond to this statement? In what way might one begin to "confess" to the earth?

CHAPTER FIVE

Sacrifice and Grace

THOMAS BERRY PRESENTS his final summation of a new theology for the present age. It is a theology with a great deal of responsibility for us all. At this moment in evolutionary history, we are called to achieve something new in behalf of the earth community, and, as with all the great moments in the history of the universe's achievements, it will have its moments of great sacrifice.

Ignatius of Loyola, founder of the Roman Catholic Jesuit order, leads Thomas Clarke to special reflections on the gift of grace. In this chapter, Clarke puts these notions of grace within the context of the ecological age.

Both Thomas Berry and Thomas Clarke share their communitarian, theological, and "cosmic" selves in a special way in these concluding remarks.

THOMAS BERRY

The Context

Sacrifice

We are at a period of change that I have described as the transition from a terminal Cenozoic era to the emerging Ecozoic era. This transition is an integral part of the great journey of the universe that emerged in the beginning in such a wonderful flaring

131

forth of what is sometimes designated as "the fireball." I call it a primordial flaring forth of life and existence. If everything that exists now was contained in the possibilities of the original moment—our "infolded" mode of being—we are the "unfolded" mode of being of that primordial flaring forth. It has been a great journey and it is why it is important to ritualize this, to enact it, and to tell the story. It is not simply telling the story, however, but also bringing about in the process one of the momentous transitions in the story.

The universe story is the account of a long sequence of transformations. In some ways, all that has gone before is imperiled at our moment of the story and we are asked to undertake a vast transformation to enable the next phase of the story to come into being. We are venturing into a truly new type experience. It requires a great deal of us. We did not choose to be here; the story selected us to be here. Once we are here, we must be willing to fulfil the destiny assigned to us; that is our grandeur, that is our blessedness, that is our joy, that is our peace. That is our gift to the great community of existence that is making the journey as a single sacred community. We are not making the journey simply by ourselves. We are making it with the entire universe community, the human community, the life community, the earth community. It is a single journey. At different moments, special responsibilities are assigned to specific groups of people. Each of us, in our separate ways, is destined to be a significant personality in celebrating the past, grieving over the disasters of the present, and giving birth to the future.

All the great transition moments are sacrificial moments. Our present transition will not be accomplished without enormous sacrifice. Regarding the supernova explosions, where the temperature of the first generation stars was intensified so fantastically that the heavier elements could be formed, and then exploded out into the universe, a person might say that the first generation stars underwent that self-sacrificial moment in order that everything afterward could come into existence.

Sacrifice is the idea that whatever is achieved has a price. Something is given, and a response is made. Parents give to their children and what is the recompense of the children? The recompense is recognition of the parents. There is an asymmetry between the gift and the response. They are not always of the same order. Persons are given a physical gift. They do not necessarily have to give a physical gift in return. They can give the gift of gratitude. The thing that exists in our times and the root of the tragedy might be considered to be our unwillingness to make the return for what has been given us; the entire industrial system is an effort to bypass the return, the price to be paid for our present comforts. We are trying to take from the earth without giving to the earth. It is that simple. We are taking beneficial resources and giving back poisonous products.

This idea of a return to be made is universally recognized. Confucius (551–479 B.C.) was the first public teacher of early China, the great guide, the great creative personality of that period. He was a remarkably gracious person. He is one of the few great leaders who combined gentility, graciousness, and a sense of the ordinary with this grandeur. The remarkable thing about the *Analects* of Confucius is that these little sayings are so ordinary and apparently so trivial. Whereas the Bible opens with this grand creation of the universe, the *Analects* of Confucius simply says, "How wonderful it is to greet friends from afar, sit down together, and converse." Who would ever think of beginning a great work by simply saying that it is a great event when friends come from afar to sit down and speak together? Confucius was a teacher and he traveled a lot and spoke a lot, and of course students are always listening to teachers talking. So his students one day came to him and said, "You tell us a lot of things; couldn't you say them more simply?" Confucius said, "I will do that. I'll give you a single word that will sum up everything. Reciprocity." This is the bonding, the giving, the receiving—reciprocity.

This is why we have sacrifice. We have been given the universe. In recognition of this gift, we undertake a denial of something in order to recognize that we need to give something in return, but there is nothing that we have to give in return, in an ultimate sense, except what we were given. So we give something back in return as sacrifice. It is self-sacrifice that makes the universe possible. Every living being is sacrificed for other living beings. We will eventually be sacrificed for the small bacterial forms that will consume us. That is the sacrifice that we are going to make. Everything feeds on other beings and nourishes other beings. The grass is fed by the sun and the sun is fed by the energies inherent in the supernova explosion of the star, whence our sun is derived, and so back to the primordial blazing forth. All this enables us to feed on the grass. Fed by each other, we nourish each other. The universe is caught up in this reciprocity. It has a sacrificial dimension.

The significance of sacrifice is determined by the situation's order of magnitude. The sacrifice of the first generation stars was of the order of magnitude that would make the planet earth possible. We are born out of the sacrifice of a first generation star. Correspondingly, with our times, there are sacrifices to be made. There is the sacrifice of so many of those things that we think are owed to us. The problem is that we feel the blessings we have are things we have a right to, that it is an unjust world if we do not have a superabundance; it is an unjust world if we do not have air conditioning in the summer and an abundance of heat in the winter. A certain sacrifice is involved as we give up some of our conveniences. The entire industrial world must now enter into a sacrificial phase. If this happens, the economy will decline. People must relinquish jobs in an industrial context and assume roles in an ecological context. Indeed, transforming something, the dismantling and the rebuilding, reshaping, or reforming of things, is certainly more difficult than initially bringing the thing into being.

So, at the present time, the reshaping of the human face of the planet, the reshaping of our economy, the reshaping of our education, law, religious orientations, and so forth, is not going to be without its negative, sacrificial, entropic aspects. But these are what we must willingly undertake. This sense of sacrifice must enter into our thought and activity. We have been trying to bargain for the future, but we cannot in reality bargain for the new thing to be born. The first generation stars did not bargain over what they were doing. The first generation stars performed their historical role in bringing about the order of things which resulted from their self-sacrifice. We cannot bargain with life. It is a pure gift. There are things to be done even though death is involved, and what is very hard is that sometimes we are called upon not only to undergo the death transformation ourselves. We have to ask it of each other, and that does not come easily.

But there is another important thing, the birth of new modes of being. We must enter into this with an attraction and a joy and a delight because this is a supreme opportunity being offered us. This is our glory. This is the magnificence of being chosen to be alive at the present time, to be chosen among the first to enter into this new mode of consciousness. One of the difficulties with the entire environmental movement is a pervasive lack of understanding of just how deep the movement has to go to be authentic. If we consider any of the historical movements that have taken place, we find that they all had their archetypal, sacrificial personalities. People are effective precisely to the extent to which they enter into the sacrificial mode.

The sacrificial mode itself can be explained in a rather understandable way in terms of the different selves that we have. We have our personal self, our family self, our earth self, and our universe self. We have many selves. A tree is a living being; it is an earth being, a universe being. Every being has a universal context. Sacrifice, ultimately, is the choice of the larger self, because when the larger self is endangered by the smaller self, the smaller self must give way to the larger self when it is in its authentic mode. What we are being asked is to choose our larger self. Our larger self is located there in the Ecozoic. That is our larger self. Being born into the Ecozoic era is the process that we are undertaking.

We might say that we are into a phase of midwifery, that is, a phase of birthing the new structure of the planet earth. We ourselves need to be reborn, the earth needs to be reborn. We are in the process. It is our historical role. It is the purpose of our present conversation.

It is our hope, as we go forth being mystically present to each other and supportive of each other. Wherever we gather, we will have a feeling that something is happening, that this is a destiny that is ours, that the Ecozoic era prepared by former generations is being called into being not only by ourselves, but also, in a mysterious way, by future generations. Our hope is that the work we are doing, demanding as it is, is succeeding, and that we are on our way to a grand, celebratory phase of the earth, of life, of the human community—a new phase in the story of the universe.

The Issues

Free Choice

Both destiny and free choice are elements in every situation. We did not ask to be born in this century. We did not ask to have blue eyes or brown eyes or to have a certain figure or to have certain emotional responses. We did not ask to be genetically coded precisely by the genetic process that brought us into being individually, and which carries our destiny to a large extent. To be born in some other time, we would not be who we are. To be born in some other situation, we would not be who we are. So destiny and free choice are both inherent elements. Of course, it was the free choice of parents to be married, but that also has an element of determinism. We are determining the destinies of each other at every moment and also shaping our own destiny, but it all goes together in a deep mystery.

If we think back over our lives, most of us can see how by something happening, by turning a corner, or meeting a person, life is changed. Missing something by a fraction of a couple of seconds may determine our lives from that moment on. We pick up something to read and our lives are different. Lives are shaped moment to moment by every single thing that happens. I think most of us have been given so many things that other peoples have not been given. It is a humbling thing to look back over the things we have been given. I would say it is destiny and choice, but choice involves the possibility of betraying destiny. There is also the possibility of confirming the opportunity granted us. It must, however, be enacted freely. We have the choice to be true to the gifts we are given.

I would insist that the gifts we are given are not simply, and perhaps not primarily, for ourselves. They are certainly not simply for our personal selves. The gifts are for our larger self, for the role that we have in the larger community of things. That, to my mind, is the reason for the gifts we are given. That is why nature diversifies. As Thomas Aquinas says in a beautiful passage, "So that the perfection lacking to one would be supplied by the other." We are supplying the perfection lacking in one another. What we do not have as individuals is enormously greater than what we do have. We need *all* the people around us, we need everyone, we need every leaf on every tree, we need every earthworm in the earth, we need every bacterial reality, every microbe and every event. We need everything. The community is the larger reality, our larger personal destiny. Yet the community depends on the integral development of each individual.

Women and Sacrifice

I should enlarge my treatment of individual and communal sacrifice in terms of the fact that we cannot do anything unless we are something personally. So many friendships and so many marriages fail, I think, because there is an emptiness, there is no capacity to give or receive. Individual talents need to be fully developed, certainly the personal development of women and their achieving their rightful place in society are of primary concern.

A sense of sacrifice can be disastrous if it is not understood properly. I think it is quite proper to bring out the danger inherent in the idea of sacrifice. It can be very disruptive, there is no doubt of that. We need to have a strong, personal self, and that is why the "courage to be" is so important, as Paul Tillich (1886–1965) said. The courage to be our individual selves is enormously important. We cannot fulfill the role of our larger selves without fulfilling our personal selves, our personal destiny. That is one of the finer things that everyone needs to be aware of. It takes courage to be the person that each of us is, the courage to be unique, different, and assertive in fulfilling our personal destiny, our personal role.

THOMAS CLARKE

The Context

I would like to start by expressing my deepest thanks to everyone, to Tom Berry and to all involved in this conversation. Through you, I thank the divine for such a remarkable experience. I attended a workshop on ecology by Paula Gonzalez of the Inter-Community Justice and Peace Center in Cincinnati. Paula talked about the exchange of water molecules which takes place continually in our human contact. Of course we do not own those molecules. I know that I will be carrying off so many water molecules, and I know I will continue to drink from that living water which we share. In reflecting on this I pondered on the theme which we have not explicated and that is the theme of grace. My reflections brought me back to three or four particular points of reference in the story of grace as I have experienced it. I will briefly mention these.

The Issues

Ignatian Insights

The first one is from my Jesuit heritage. At the very end of the *Spiritual Exercises*, Ignatius of Loyola suggests a "Contemplation for Gaining Divine Love," and he begins by saying that love consists in a mutual self-giving, in communication. (It is interesting that Karl Rahner, a Jesuit, centers his whole theology around this notion of the self-communication of God to the created world, and everything in Rahner's vision is related to that.) In the Contemplation, Ignatius develops four points: gift, presence, labor, and sacrament. He asks us first to contemplate the many gifts of God and then how, in those gifts, there is the self-giving of God. The appropriate response is total self-giving. This is where, of course, you have the famous Ignatian prayer, "Take and Receive," in which we offer our freedom.

Ignatius then moves into what would be a kind of ecological pre-history where he talked about God as present in the gifts. In the rather scholastic way of his time, he specifies the levels of creation—the inanimate, the vegetative, the animal, and the human—and discusses how God dwells in all of these. It seems to me that this is the kind of transformation of the *Spiritual Exercises* we Jesuits now really have to undertake. I think that this is a special point to work with, especially in terms of the Holy Spirit as God radically immanent in the total creation.

I hope this is not just appropriating or capturing something which I should really let be on its own for awhile, but one of the things I want to work with is *Gaia* and Spirit. Is *Gaia*, in this ultimate divine dimension, really that self gift of God, God as gift, the most radical aspect of the cosmogenesis? If we could look at the relationship between *Gaia* and the Holy Spirit in a new way, the Holy Spirit as a feminine dimension of God, and the earth mother in its deepest aspect—that would give me tremendous joy. I know that would energize me tremendously.

The third point has to do with labor; this is an echo of that passage in St. Paul about how the Spirit is in "the groaning" of creation. Ignatius has us contemplate how God, as it were, labors in the whole universe. (I think Teilhard must have gotten a good deal of his inspiration from that call to struggle.) And now, of course, it is the struggle not to win souls (which was the Ignatian language), but the struggle to join the earth's community in the healing of this relationship. On Ignatius's last point, I like to use the term "sacrament"; you could also perhaps say "ecstasy." But, he says, having contemplated the gift, the presence, the labor, we might see all of these gifts as rays coming from the sun or as waters cascading down from a hidden fountain. And he is asking us to say, "What is God like? What is the divine?" This is one of the things I think I have begun to learn, that the new cosmology in these terms is saying: "Don't skip those first three points; don't be in too much of a rush to get to point four, or to go beyond. Be willing to linger with gift and presence and labor. Don't try to manipulate cosmogenesis and don't get out of touch. Don't think that you have to leave the world or earth to find God."

That was the first reference point for me. I also thought of Augustine and his struggle, the whole question of grace, and so on. And I thought of a recent book by Peruvian theologian Gustavo Gutiérrez, a very moving book, *On Job* (Maryknoll, New York: Orbis, 1987), in which the struggle of Job with God is orchestrated. Gutiérrez is wondering how we can speak of God today in the context of the suffering of the innocent. For us, concerned as we are with the earth, the innocent are the other members of the earth community who have suffered such violence at our hands. That is the kind of context in which we have to ask, "What is God like? How do we talk about God?"

A Life-Giving Banquet

The final point of reference that I would like to mention is the movie *Babette's Feast*. In the film, you have the contrast between this very tight, life-denying, aging religious sect, and this woman, Babette, a culinary artist who comes in as a refugee from the French Revolution. The drama unfolds within this contrast between the attitudes of this religious sect and her approach to life, her generosity and her sense of the gratuity of life. At the end of the film, she crystallizes it all by saying, "All over the world, the voice of the artist is heard: let me do my best."

The whole movie revolves around a fabulous meal that she prepares and serves, and how the meal transforms this community. The only one who really understands what is happening is a general who earlier on had the possibility of a romance with one of the two spinster daughters. Both of the daughters, when young, in a fleeting moment, had a chance for self-giving love, but because of the self-denying and the life-denying community, they could not respond. I will conclude by quoting what the general says:

Man, my friends, is frail and foolish. We have all of us been told that grace is to be found in the universe [in the movie version, it says "mercy," but in the short story of Isak Dinesen on which it is based, the term "grace" is used], but in our human foolishness and shortsightedness, we imagine divine grace to be finite. For this reason, we tremble. We tremble before making our choice in life, and, after having made it, again tremble in fear of having chosen wrong. But the moment comes when our eyes are opened and we see and realize that grace is infinite. Grace demands nothing from us but that we shall await it with confidence and acknowledge it with gratitude. Grace makes no conditions and singles out none of us in particular. Grace takes us all into its bosom and proclaims general amnesty. That which we had chosen is given us, that which we have refused is also and at the same time granted us. Aye, that which we have rejected is poured out on us abundantly. For mercy and truth have met together and righteousness and truth have kissed one another.

QUESTIONS FOR REFLECTION AND DISCUSSION

1. How do you respond to Berry's emphasis on, and understanding of, sacrifice? Challenging? Threatening? To what extent

do you agree with the statement that "all the great transition moments are sacrificial moments"?

2. By encouraging self-sacrifice, do you think Berry is contributing, in a negative way, to the traditional (and oppressive) self-sacrificing role of women? Why or why not?

3. Does Berry's overall theological vision cohere for you? What do you find challenging or missing in his theology?

4. What is your response to Thomas Clarke's conclusion that we do not have to leave the earth in order to find God? Where, in this ecological framework, do we find God?

5. How do you think Clarke's treatment of grace helps the understanding of the new context of theology? What does grace mean in this new context? Where is it found?

Appendix

The following material is Thomas Berry's response to a question about his personal involvement in the ecological question. It is followed by a request from several native persons from the Six Nations near Brantford, Ontario, who came to the Colloquium to meet Thomas Berry.

The Roots of Thomas Berry

I have always lived marginally. My mother told me once that I was so difficult as a child, that by the age of four, my mother and father had a conference one day about me, and my father said, "We have been nice and sweet and kind to this boy. We have spanked him, we have punished him. Just nothing's going to work. I guess he will just have to raise himself."

There seem to be deep, personal gifts or determinations that each of us has. This sense of a certain distance from what was officially happening has never bothered me. I went my way and tried to keep a certain independence. It is one of the reasons why I began to study the Asian world, learned the Chinese language, and learned Sanskrit. I studied history and philosophy to find out and to test out how people found meaning. I wanted to go back through the whole human tradition and test the whole process, because it was obvious from the beginning, going into religious life, that the process was not working. Just like now, our modern world is not working. Christianity, in this sense, is not working. Particularly, there is the inability of the Christian world to respond in any effective way to the destruction of the planet. Religion is assuming no responsibility for the state of the earth or the fate of the earth. Although, as I mentioned, there is a concern for suicide, homicide, genocide, there is this terrible lack of concern for biocide or geocide. We have no moral principles to deal with them.

Somehow, when I was quite young, I saw the beginnings of biocide and genocide. By the time I was nine, I had collected a number of catalogues concerning life in the distant forests of the American Northwest. I figured the only way you escaped from the emerging industrial world was go to the northwestern U.S., and so I collected from several publications such as *Boys' Life* the addresses of companies supplying camping equipment. I collected catalogues advertising the canoes that I would need and the equipment and the knives and all the other items that were needed to go to the wilderness. I saw the wilderness-civilization issue, or I felt it, and was acting on it.

The most difficult thing I have had in my whole life is reconciling myself to the existent order of things and living among the ambivalences that we live in. We cannot survive without ambivalence, and that is where the capacity to sustain ambivalence seems to be the quintessential thing. We need the capacity to sustain the ambivalence of the religious structure without abandoning it, the ambivalence of our society without abandoning it, the ambivalences of the automobile—and I am ready to abandon that—and the airports. I think we all have these sensitivities. I think children have it all the time. We get educated out of it. So it was not anything special, I guess, with myself, but I tried to create the distance. I do not know how I got through religious life, or training, because I kept a distance between myself and the establishment all the way, although to this day I live within a religious community.

These instincts are deep in us. We feel that things need to be done. We are groping our way. There is this problem of how we manage some of these things. But we do not have any more time. There is no time, in regard to the planet, the ecosystem, and the rain forest. We do not have time. We have got to act, and how to act is the difficulty and that is why the work that is being done in this discussion has such great urgency, because we do not have time. In the church, the theological development has to be now. We cannot wait and let things just spin off into increasing devastation. The present failure of the church to assume its religious responsibility for the fate of the earth is, without a doubt, the greatest failure in the course of Christian history.

Things are happening, though. We have a special opportunity across the board in economics. Even the U.S. Army Corps of Engineers has changed. (If they can change, just about anything can change.) They have recognized that building all the dams, disturbing the natural world, and trying to re-engineer the North American continent has been a disasterous mistake. Now they must begin to heal the things they can save.

I have a feeling that, from here on, those committed to the ecological issue, those committed to the renewal of the planet, are in charge. In a sense, we are in charge now. We are in charge theologically. We are in charge economically. We are in charge politically. Nothing is going to happen politically, or economically, except under the sign of being ecologically sound. Politicians will have to proclaim themselves ecologists. All the corporations have to stress their ecological concerns. Even General Motors just took out a big ad, in *The New York Times*, about their special contributions to environmental protection. So we are in a situation where things are happening, but we have got to act with clarity and decisiveness.

I have this problem in my native state, North Carolina, which I call a Third World state. (We do have Third World states in the U. S.) But where I grew up is a wonderful area. During the late teens and twenties of this century, it was such a beautiful region. But then there was the rise of industrialization. The beginnings of a manufacturing economy came after the Civil War when the South was defeated, and that destruction continued up pretty much through the nineteenth century and into this century when I came along in 1914. I got some of the feeling of economic recovery, and not only recovery, but of people committing themselves to the industrial world and seeking its benefits. North Carolina has outdone many other states in one thing: building roads. We have more state supported roads than any other state. And still, out of a meager budget, North Carolina's legislature just passed a bill providing $9 billion for more highways, whereas it subtracted heavily from basic education, which shows a commitment to the industrial world.

Yet there is no ideal for North Carolina to follow. There is no single ideal community. Cerro Gardo in Northern California is constituting a community, a sustaining village community, with their craft skills, their relationship to the land, their giving up of the automobile for the bicycle. What we need are such diverse community models. We have communities with religious dimensions, intentional communities, but I do not think that they will be prevalent in the future. We need communities in the civic order— sustainable, meaningful communities that have a sense of the sacred dimension of existence, a sense of the sacred that would not be sectarian. There needs to be provision for a society in which there are a diversity of spiritual directions. What we now have are mainly industrial-based communities.

In North Carolina, we have the Triangle Research Center. It is the glory of the state now, where thirty of the biggest industrial corporations in the U.S. put their research on a 5000 acre area. It is killing the region. They say it makes jobs.

I go down and I object to the research center. I critique the road building. I critique the whole idea of bringing in outside industrial companies for the sake of making jobs. North Carolina people live rurally, although they work in factories for the most part or in commercial establishments. I am trying to get the North Carolina people to see that the grandeur of the region in its natural splendor is being devastated by all this industrial development. I go down and I say, "You start off now with this big, prestigious research center. Then you have to build these thousands of homes, expensive homes, for the high-paid people. Then you have to change the streets to handle the traffic. You have to change the water system. You have to change the waste disposal system. You must have new water supplies. Then you have to build this vast, new international airport. Then new schools must be built, new social services, new medical facilities. And so it goes, on and on until the entire region is swallowed up by development."

You see, that is not the genius of the place. The genius of North Carolina is its mountains, its wonderful Piedmont section, its wonderful coastal plain and its sea coast, all fertile regions. We need to understand this region. What we need is an appropriate culture for this area. Are we so incompetent that we cannot set up an internal economy? Are we so lacking in mental creativity that we cannot create our art and our poetry and our music? They do this in many places in the mountains of North Carolina. We need to create a people who are educated for life here. North Carolina is at the bottom of the list of states in SAT (Scholastic Aptitude Test) scores, which are the scores for admission into college, but I say we do not need SAT scores.

What we need are people who are happy people, who are creative people, who have their music, their culture, in relationship to these fantastic resources that exist. There is no reason to feel ashamed of our villages or our cities simply because they are not industrialized. Our destiny is to develop a truly human life and culture in these villages and cities. It would take a long time to outline precisely what I have in mind concerning community life and culture in North Carolina. Essentially, what I am suggesting is a complex of communities of different sizes living out of the resources and the inspiration of their region.

Request from Members of the Six Nations

Something that is tied in with the earth is that there should be an abandonment of the policy of assimilation; this is one thing you could do to help us. What we have here are traditional people from the Six Nations and we are having a problem. One concern we have is the Martyrs' Shrine in Midland, Ontario, run by the Jesuits and another shrine in Auriesville, New York, also run by Jesuits. And that continual put-down of our image to the general public is hurting us. (The Shrines commemorate Jesuit missionaries killed by native Americans.) It has hurt us. It continues to hurt us because, as long as you have got the martyrs, "the good guy" martyrs, you have to have "the bad guys." We have historically been portrayed by the Jesuits as the bad guys and they are using language and feelings that existed at the time that the Jesuit *Relations* were written over 300 years ago. They are still using those same words today and expressing those same feelings about our people. And I am sure that the minds of hundreds and thousands and maybe millions of people who have gone through those places have been poisoned against us. This is a concern for us. It should not exist, and if there are people here who want something to sink their teeth into, something worthwhile, maybe you could help us in our struggle with the Jesuits.

Glossary

Anthropic principle. In its strong form, the anthropic principle states that the conditions of the early universe made life inevitable in the further evolution of the universe.

Analogy. A comparison of two things that have a similar function but are different in structure and origin. (Analogy is used in comparative anatomy, but also in philosophical discourse.)

Biocentrism. The view that the entire life community must be considered in human planning; similar to *geocentrism*, which suggests that the entire earth must be similarly considered. These are contrasted with *anthropocentrism*, the view that humans are separate and above the rest of life and the cosmos, and of overriding concern.

Bioregions. Areas of the earth established on a functional community basis, that is, generally self-sustaining regions with mutually supporting life-systems.

Cenozoic. The era of geological history from 65 million years ago to the present, marked by the rapid evolution of mammals, birds, grasses, shrubs, and higher flowering plants.

Complexity-centration. A Teilhardian term, indicating the gradual evolution through the ages toward more complexity of life, and, at the same time, a greater "inwardness."

Cosmogenesis. The current scientific understanding that the universe is not "being" but always in the process of "becoming."

Docetism. From early Christian history, a belief, opposed as heretical, that Jesus only *seemed* to have a human body and to suffer and die on the cross.

Ecozoic. A term coined by Thomas Berry to indicate the need for a new era of mutually-enhancing human-earth relationships. He contrasts this future with the *technozoic*, a future dream of overcoming the limits and basic rhythms and conditions of the planet with technology.

Emergent universe. An understanding of the universe as unfolding and open to new possibilities as this happens.

Epistemology. The study of the nature and grounds of knowledge.

Immanence. Remaining or operating within the universe. In Christian theology generally, it is used in reference to God but is different from pantheism, that is, the total identification of God with the universe.

Macrophase/microphase. The large and the small dimension of everything. An example used by Thomas Berry is that, while a single automobile is quite harmless to the biosphere, the worldwide use of millions of them constitutes a threat to the planet. Similarly, humans, as a limited species and in the present numbers, are two different realities for the planet. This differentiation is necessary for moving to a sense of the larger dimensions of ethics.

New Story. A term also coined by Thomas Berry referring to the present, scientific understanding of the cosmos as developing and inter-connected by origin. While science has developed the physical meaning of this, Berry seeks to have us understand this as a sacred story of the universe and of the total human venture.

Ontology. A branch of metaphysics concerned with the nature of being.

Pelagian. Relating to the beliefs of Pelagius (360?–420 A.D), who denied the existence of original sin and emphasized the perfectibility of humans without grace. In the mainstream of Christian theology, this is considered a heresy.

Spatial mode of consciousness. This consciousness sees the universe as fixed and unchanging, in contrast to a time-developmental understanding.

Transcendence. Prior to or above the universe. Thomas Berry uses it analogously to refer to, for example, technology that knows no restraint from the natural systems of the planet.

Bibliography

Editor's Note: For a more extensive bibliography, we suggest readers consult the following five sources:

Berry, Thomas. *The Dream of the Earth.* San Francisco: Sierra Club Books, 1988.

Berry, Thomas. *Riverdale Papers.* Riverdale Center, 5801 Palisade Ave., Bronx, N.Y., 10471. A collection of volumes of Berry's published and unpublished essays.

Lonergan, Anne and Caroline Richards. *Thomas Berry and the New Cosmology.* Mystic, Connecticut: Twenty-Third Publications, 1987. An excellent primer on Christian ecology.

McDaniel, Jay. *Earth, Sky, Gods, & Mortals: Developing an Ecological Christianity.* Mystic, Connecticut: Twenty-Third Publications, 1990. Builds an ecological spirituality from process theology. Includes one of the best bibliographies on ecological theology.

Teilhard Studies. American Teilhard Association, Box 67, White Plains, N.Y. 10604. A series of scholarly monographs on the significance of Teilhard. Several in the series are by Berry, including "Teilhard in the Ecological Age."

For Further Reading

Birch, Charles., William Eakin, and Jay McDaniel, eds. *Liberating Life: Contemporary Approaches to Ecological Theology.* Maryknoll, N.Y.: Orbis Books, 1990. A wide-ranging collection of theological essays from varied traditions, prepared for the 1991 General Assembly of World Council of Churches. Solid overview of ecological theology at present, and its relationship to liberation theology.

Bookchin, Murray, *The Philosophy of Social Ecology: Essays in Dialectical Naturalism*. Montreal: Black Rose, 1990. Although Bookchin is approaching the relationship between humans and the rest of the earth in a very different way than Berry, he stresses the continuity of differentiation, subjectivity, and freedom.

Dowd, Michael. *Earthspirit: A Handbook for Nurturing an Ecological Christianity*. Mystic, Connecticut: Twenty-Third Publications, 1991. A good, clean introduction to Berry and the new story.

Griffin, David Ray, ed. *The Reenchantment of Science*. Albany: State University of New York Press, 1988. This first in a fine series on post-modern thinking in various areas includes science, theology, philosophy, spirituality and art. It is profound and clearly presented.

McDonagh, Sean. *To Care for the Earth: A Call to A New Theology*. Santa Fe, N.M.: Bear and Company, 1987. A development of Berry's theology, written by a Columban missioner in South Mindanao in the Philippines.

Moore, Thomas, ed. *A Blue Fire: Selected Readings of James Hillman*. New York: Harper & Row, 1989. These selections from a Jungian psychotherapist constitute an impassioned call to return "soul" to the world of things. In many ways, his vision complements Berry's on our various "selves," e.g., family, community, and cosmic.

Morowitz, Harold J. *Cosmic Joy and Local Pain: Musings of A Mystic Scientist*. New York: Charles Scribner's, 1987. Morowitz, a professor of molecular biophysics and biochemistry, explores the dynamism of the earth, air, water, fire in the interconnectedness of this planet, and includes a fine, appreciative chapter on Teilhard.

Palmer, Martin. *Genesis or Nemesis: Belief, Meaning, and Ecology*. London: Dryad Press, 1988. A strong argument for the need for radical change in worldviews in order to deal with the ecological crisis.

Van Buren, Paul M. "Covenantal Pluralism?" *Cross Currents*, Vol. 40, No. 3, Fall 1990. An imaginative approach to covenant that argues for the differentiation of revelation to all peoples, rather than the narrow exclusivity rejected by Berry.

Vittachi, Anuradha. *Earth Conference One: Sharing a Vision for Our Planet.* Boston: New Science Library, Shambhala, 1989. This is an eye-witness account of the Global Survival Conference in Oxford, 1988, where Thomas Berry, as well as other religious and political representatives, clarified many significant issues.

Index

Also available from Twenty-Third Publications: a 13-part video series, *Befriending the Earth,* on which this book is based. It features the actual footage between Thomas Berry and Thomas Clarke.

Part I	Healing Theology
Part II	From Science to the Sacred
Part III	Knowing God
Part IV	Falling in Love with the Universe
Part V	Sacred World
Part VI	Tragedy Is Not Our Business
Part VII	If Jesus Is Who He Says He Is, He'll Show Up Somewhere
Part VIII	Social Justice, Earth Justice
Part IX	All Creation Groaning
Part X	Terror and Attraction
Part XI	For Our Children, a Shameful Legacy
Part XII	A Song for Our Times
Part XIII	Sacrifice and Grace